Selections from the Gospel of Sri Ramakrishna

Other books in the
SkyLight Illuminations Series

Bhagavad Gita: Annotated & Explained
The Way of the Pilgrim: Annotated & Explained
The Gospel of Thomas: Annotated & Explained
Zohar: Annotated & Explained
Dhammapada: Annotated & Explained

Selections from the Gospel of Sri Ramakrishna

Annotated & Explained

Originally recorded in Bengali
by M, a disciple of the Master

Translation by
Swami Nikhilananda

Annotation by
Kendra Crossen Burroughs

Foreword by Andrew Harvey

Walking Together, Finding the Way
SKYLIGHT PATHS Publishing
Woodstock, Vermont

Library of Congress Cataloging-in-Publication Data

Ramakrishna, 1836–1886.
[Kathâmôrta. English. Selections]
Selections from the gospel of Sri Ramakrishna : annotated & explained / translation by Swami Nikhilananda ; annotation by Kendra Crossen Burroughs ; foreword by Andrew Harvey.
     p. cm.
1. Ramakrishna Mission. 2. Mysticism—Hinduism. 3. Hinduism—Doctrines. I. Nikhilânanda, Swami. II. Burroughs, Kendra Crossen. III. Title.
BL1280.292.R36 A25 2002
294.5'55'092—dc21

                                  2002001128

10 9 8 7 6 5 4 3 2 1

Manufactured in the United States of America

SkyLight Paths, "Walking Together, Finding the Way," and colophon are trademarks of LongHill Partners, Inc., registered in the U.S. Patent and Trademark Office.

Walking Together, Finding the Way
Published by SkyLight Paths Publishing
A Division of LongHill Partners, Inc.
Sunset Farm Offices, Route 4, P.O. Box 237
Woodstock, VT 05091
Tel: (802) 457-4000   Fax: (802) 457-4004
www.skylightpaths.com

Wherever you are
is the entry point.

—*Kabir*

মাস্টার—ঈশ্বরকে কি দর্শন করা যায় ?

শ্রীরামকৃষ্ণ—হাঁ, অবশ্য করা যায়। মাঝে মাঝে নির্জন বাস; তাঁর নাম গুণগান, বস্তু-বিচার; এইসব উপায় অবলম্বন করতে হয়।

মাস্টার—কি অবস্থাতে তাঁর দর্শন হয় ?

শ্রীরামকৃষ্ণ—ব্যাকুল হয়ে কাঁদলে দর্শন হয়। লোকে স্ত্রী পুত্রের জন্য এক ঘটি কাঁদে; টাকার জন্য লোকে কত কেঁদে অভিষেকের ধেয়; কিন্তু ঈশ্বরের জন্য কে কাঁদে ? ডাকার মত ডাকতে হয়।

A portion of The Gospel of Sri Ramakrishna *in the original Bengali script*

Contents □

Foreword by Andrew Harvey ix
Preface xix
Introduction xxi

1. He Was Talking of God 2
2. Keep Holy Company 10
3. God Is in the Tiger 18
4. Knowledge of Brahman 30
5. Worldly Duties 48
6. A Feast of Joy 56
7. "Where Is My Krishna?" 62
8. Play of the Divine Mother 70
9. Dive Deep 84
10. The Spirit of Renunciation 104
11. "I Am the Servant of God" 110
12. Realizing God 122
13. Beyond Good and Evil 126
14. A Yearning Heart 130
15. What Is the Way? 136
16. Reading, Hearing, and Seeing 146
17. Desire 152
18. Practicing the Disciplines 156

19. Divine Incarnation 162

20. To Receive God's Grace 166

21. Something Special 174

22. Mad with Love 186

23. "What a Vision!" 192

Notes 199

Suggested Readings 203

List of Special Terms 205

About SkyLight Paths 208

Foreword ☐

Andrew Harvey

If I had to choose one book to take with me to a desert island to contemplate for the rest of my life, or pick one book to give to a seeker today to help guide him or her into the joys and mysteries of the mystical life, it would be the one whose SkyLight Illuminations version you are now holding in your hands—*The Gospel of Sri Ramakrishna*. It was written in Bengali at the beginning of the twentieth century by Mahendra Gupta, a high school headmaster from Calcutta, under the pseudonym M. It's a precise, poignant, breathtakingly natural and candid account of a part of the life and teachings of his beloved master Sri Ramakrishna, whose life (1836–1886), lived mostly in the compound of a Kali temple by the side of the Ganges, revolutionized religious history.

The Gospel of Sri Ramakrishna is the mystical equivalent of Boswell's *Life of Dr. Johnson*: it is far more than a biography; it is a kind of living transmission of the essence of the man himself, a "conjuration" of his flaming living presence that time and cultural distance can never dim. Swami Nikhilananda, whose English translation of the *Gospel* was first published in 1942, considered these the first recorded words of the spiritual history of the world, of a man recognized as belonging in the class of a Buddha or a Christ. To read *The Gospel of Sri Ramakrishna* is to enter into a dance with the great mystic; with the One constantly driving him on; and, perhaps most mysteriously and challengingly of all, a dance with your own hidden innermost self, revealed in one of its wildest and most generous incarnations. No one who meets with their whole being the small brown man with the short beard and half-shut, obliquely set eyes that these pages celebrate will ever be the same.

I first encountered this small man who has changed my life and influenced every step of my journey in the profoundest way when I was twenty-five. I can still remember the afternoon on which I began to read M's book. I was seated at a table in a small hut by the sea in Pondicherry, in South India, gazing out at the sun shimmering in explosions of heat on the water. I had escaped the cage of an Oxford fellowship to return to drink deep from the springs of my Indian childhood and try to recover from the radiation of years of intellectual futility and emotional despair. Just two weeks before, I had undergone the first three of a series of mystical experiences that had shattered everything that I had ever understood or been taught about reality: I had been left charred, profoundly afraid that I would lose my mind. And then a friend handed me *The Gospel of Sri Ramakrishna* and told me to read it immediately. "You will find in this book everything you will ever need. You are not going mad, you are going sane."

I started reading the *Gospel* around noon; at seven, as fragrant night fell over the sea, I was still reading, transfixed and strangely calm. I was far from understanding, of course, much of what I read, but I knew that in Ramakrishna, I had met the most tender and most amazing friend, someone whose wisdom and perception would always be ready to encourage my own. In beginning to read the work of another great Hindu mystic, Aurobindo, I had already started to open tentatively to a wholly new (to me) vision of God as Mother; now, reading and experiencing Ramakrishna, I realized with awe and delight that the meaning of my whole life would be connected to the vision of the Mother I met in and through him. I realized too that, as I deepened my experience of the Mother, I would also deepen my experience of Ramakrishna, of what he had been and done and of what he was still doing to and in the heart of humanity. When I put down the *Gospel* toward midnight, too exhausted to continue, I knew that everything had changed forever for me.

Nine years later, after I had read and reread *The Gospel of Sri Ramakrishna* countless times—and, inspired by it, entered into an exploration of God as Mother and of the essence of all mystical traditions—I went on pilgrimage to the place where Ramakrishna had lived, Kali Temple, in Dakshineshwar, six miles outside of Calcutta. I sat in the serene radiance of his simple room, near the Ganges, for most of the day, and then caught a bus back to Calcutta. On the bus, I began to panic. I had no real idea where my hotel was or where the bus was going. In the immense filthy labyrinth of the city I started to pray to Ramakrishna. Five minutes later, I heard a rather high-pitched voice say in accented Indian-English, "Get out now." I looked around; no one was sitting near me. I left the bus; my hotel was thirty yards away. With tears of astonishment, I understood that the small brown man had spoken directly to me and that he would always be there to guide and direct me whenever my life re-entered chaos. I tell this story here because when I have told it to those of my spiritual friends who love Ramakrishna, they answer with their own accounts of his miraculous presence and guidance. Ramakrishna is a world-teacher in the company of Jesus and Rumi and the Buddha, transcendentally alive as they are, and tangible in the heart, as a permanently empowered "emanation" of the Beloved. I have kept a photograph of him in ecstasy (the same one that is on the cover of this book) on my desk for twenty-five years and I look into his eyes every day to remind myself of what I must try, with all my fractures and differences, to become. In times of great difficulty and torment, I have found in his company inexplicable grace and peace. At a certain juncture on the path, you discover that all the great healers and teachers and mystics of humanity are waiting behind a razor-thin veil of light to meet you and help you help others. The unveiling of this mystery of communion between all lovers of God and of the world beyond time and death is one of the holiest of revelations and one of the most useful; the responsibilities of the later stages of the path would often be unfathomable and lonely without it.

There has never been a time in which humanity needed Rama-krishna's holy company and inspiration more. The next decade will decide the fate of humankind and of much of nature. Those whose eyes have been opened see that we are all heading into a whirlwind of catastrophe, war, heartbreak on the one hand, and, on the other, of unprecedented opportunities for real transformation on a massive, world-altering scale. This time will not come again in all its terrible grace; those of us who are becoming awake have no other choice but to seize it with all the strength of our sometimes-shattered hearts and minds.

I believe that the guidance, example, and vision of Ramakrishna are essential to human survival for linked reasons. They unfold a uniquely rich understanding of the power and splendor of the Divine Mother, of her all-transforming grace, and of the unity in her complete love and knowl-edge of all religions and mystical revelations. They expose a direct path to her that anyone in any culture or of any religious, economic, social, or sexual persuasion can take to her, and they make gloriously plain the abundant, fertile life she will give to all those who turn to her in adora-tion and humble trust. Ramakrishna birthed in his own heart, body, mind, and soul the New World of the Motherhood of God that is trying now to be born on a massive scale in the holocaust of history. His life, teachings, and vision are the sign that transfiguration is not poetic illusion or the last-ditch fantasy of a few mystics, but a living and breathing reality, one infi-nitely wilder, sweeter, richer, and more all-embracing than anything any previous revelations of human potential had imagined. Ramakrishna is the pioneer of the real New Age, when living divine children are nurtured by the Motherhood of God; his closeness to us in time and the astonished but precise testimony of M and his other disciples make his challenge to us inescapable. As Lex Hixon wrote in his introduction to *Great Swan: Meet-ings with Ramakrishna,* "Ramakrishna is not a quaint person from an ancient culture, representing a particular religious background, but an Ein-stein of the planetary civilization of the near future, a greenhouse for the future evolution of humanity."

That Ramakrishna became "a greenhouse for the future evolution of humanity" was entirely due—and he himself claims this—to his lifelong devotion to the Motherhood of God. Ramakrishna came to know and understand that he had a unique mission to humanity: to unfold the revelations and possibilities that lay open to all who invoke and adore the Divine Mother in any of her names or forms. From his earliest childhood, Ramakrishna had a passion for the Mother; as a boy, Swami Saradananda tells us in his *Sri Ramakrishna, the Great Master,* "Ramakrishna gave up going to school and applied his mind to the worship of the Devi. But where was peace even in that? His mind questioned, 'Is it true that the universal Mother is the embodiment of bliss and not a mere stone image? Or is it a superstition of the human mind, augmented by fond imagination and tradition of ages that has produced this unreal shadowy figure? And has man thus been deceiving himself from time immemorial?' His mind became extremely eager to solve that great problem'" (2:771).

The unfolding of his life—and of her in and through him—became the overwhelming answer to this "great problem." Not long after Ramakrishna came to live in the compound of Rani Rasmani's temple of Kali at Dakshineswar in his late teens, he began the most comprehensive journey into the Motherhood of God that the world has seen. Absolute trust in and devotion to the Mother led him from stage to stage of ecstasy, empowerment, and revelation of her nature in all its dazzling and paradoxical formal and formless aspects until, at last, he came to know her to be as inseparable from Brahman the absolute reality "as burning is from fire."

For him, the entire cosmos in all of its infinite grandeur and tiniest details became a never-ending epiphany of the Mother. Swami Saradananda reports Ramakrishna as saying, "I see as if all trees, plants, men, grass, water and other things are only sheaths of various kinds. They are like pillowcases. Have you not seen them? Some are made of coarse cotton cloth dyed red, some of chintz, and others of different kinds of cloth; and in size, some are quadrangular, others circular. The

Universe is just so ...again, just as the same thing, namely cotton, is stuffed into all these pillowcases, so that one invisible Existence-Knowledge-Bliss dwells within all the sheaths. My children, for me, it is actually as if the Mother has covered herself with wrappers of various kinds or hidden behind various forms, and is peeping out from within them all" (*Sri Ramakrishna, the Great Master,* 2:675). This revelation of the Mother in and as everything was the gift of six months of total absorption in her in 1864, when Ramakrishna was twenty-eight, in the highest, nondual bliss known as *nirvikalpa Samadhi.* In the Hindu mystical tradition, it is said that such a state destroys the body, or necessitates the soul's abandonment of its "sheath" after only three weeks; Ramakrishna was kept alive by the help of a mysterious monk who fed him the barest minimum for his body's survival. When he "came down" from this prolonged ecstasy, he was transfigured and visibly divinely empowered. The Mother herself, it is said, asked him to remain in *bhavamukha*—at the threshold of relative and absolute consciousness—so as to be able to teach, embody, and witness her reality.

It was in this extraordinary state of unity that Ramakrishna then proceeded on what remains the most revolutionary aspect of his journey: his plunging first into the depths of Islam toward the end of 1866, when, with the help of a Sufi adept, he realized union with Allah; and then, eight years later, in November 1874, his plunging into Christianity. After three days of absorption in Christ, he met and merged into him in the garden of Dakshineswar. From these two immense experiences (and those that preceded them), Ramakrishna became the first known prophet in history to proclaim the essential unity of all religions, thus pointing the way to the end of all division and war in the name of religion and pioneering a new planetary civilization, in which all faiths would be honored as complementary and distinct paths to God, different "dishes" in the heavenly and merciful cuisine of the Mother for her children. As Ramakrishna said, "God has made different religions to suit different aspirations, times and countries . . . as a mother in nursing her sick children gives rice and curry to one, and sago and arrowroot to another, and bread and butter to a third, so the Lord has laid out different paths for different people." The potential value of this vision—of all paths and revelations unified in the Mother—is incalculable; only an undivided humankind can solve the economic, political, and environmental problems that menace all life, and humankind can only be undivided if religions that are now the source of strife give up their ignorant claims of exclusiveness.

Ramakrishna did not merely experience this revelation of unity: he pointed out a direct path to its realization that beings of all cultures or belief structures could take. The fabulous richness and range of his own experience gave him inner knowledge of the many ways of approaching God, with or without form; and his own constant experience of the direct grace of the Mother convinced him that anyone who turned to her—as he had—with total trust and belief would be fed—as he had been—directly by her, with everything they would need to become her illumined servants of radical love.

This was a revolutionary position, one that implicitly challenged millennia of priestly control and guru-worship. Those who claim Ramakrishna as a guru figure limit him; he was, of course, the most magical and lucid of teachers. But he was also something more mysterious—a living, divine child of the Mother who pointed a way of direct connection to her that could help all others who sincerely and ardently wanted it to birth themselves in her. He himself hated being called a "guru," for he knew that the Mother and her inner guide within every heart are the only real "gurus," and his experience of her had taken him far beyond the need for any kind of authority, even one he claimed to be "divine"; in this way too Ramakrishna's example was prophetic. As the religious and mystical structures of authority crumble around us, Ramakrishna's discovery and embodiment of the direct path will become more and more empowering. As he said, "The substance is one under different names, and everyone is seeing the same substance: only climate, temperament and name create differences. Let each man follow his own path. If he sincerely and

ardently wishes to know God, peace be unto him, he will surely realize
him." Ramakrishna's own journey began and ended with only one
teacher: the Mother herself. On his way he embraced and learned deeply
from several adepts but ultimately absorbed and transcended all they
had to offer him. He gives all modern seekers a deathless example of the
necessary dance between respectful but not slavish dependence and fun-
damental independence in and under God that the fullest realizations
necessitate.

If Ramakrishna had only left humanity the vision of the all-unifying
Motherhood of God and the direct path to her, he would have permanently changed the religious history. But through the divine agency of his
disciple M he did something even more astonishing: he left us, in M's
pages, a permanent and excruciatingly beautiful image of the life that
abandon to the Mother brings. The ecstatic and lucid being that haunts
the pages of M's *Gospel* is someone who has fused at ever-increasing
depths of sacred truth, and passion, all possible human and divine opposites, masculine and feminine, to birth in himself the sacred Divine Child,
and to manifest the miraculous powers of clarity and rapture that dance
and keep dancing from such a birth. M's Ramakrishna is at once intensely
human and divine, at once childlike and innocent and wise-majestic. No
realm of vision is closed to him; no secret does not stand open to his
gaze, and no tenderness is beneath him. He is as much his divine self
laughing with his heart-friends on a boat or at a supper party as he is
drowned in silence or speaking with divinely inspired clarity the essential
truths of the path. There is a description of Ramakrishna dancing by
Swami Saradananda that perfectly captures the mystery of his infinitely
subtle negotiation and marriage of all levels of reality: "An extraordinary
tenderness, sweetness and leonine strength were visible in every limb of
the Master's body. That superb dance! In it there was no artificiality or
affectation, no bumping, no unnatural gestures and acrobatics; nor was
there to be noticed any absence of control. On the other hand, one
noticed in it a succession of natural poses and movements of limbs as a

gushing overflow of grace, bliss and sweetness surging from within, the like of which may be noticed in the movements of a large fish, long confined in a mud puddle when it is suddenly let loose in a vast sheet of water—swimming in all directions, now slowly, now rapidly, and expressing its joy in diverse ways. It appeared as if the dance was the dynamically bodily expression of the surge of bliss, the reality of Brahman, which the Master was experiencing within"(2:801). If we do not embody this dance of the Mother, with "extraordinary tenderness, sweetness and leonine strength" at all levels and in all institutions, the world will die out. In the sublime interconnected dance of Ramakrishna's teachings, life and vision, we are given the music we need to move to, a vision of the divine choreography that we need to reimagine for our own lives, and an eternal sign of the power of her love in us that can transform, endure, and transfigure all things.

In the unabridged version of *The Gospel of Sri Ramakrishna,* the Master describes the passion that grew in him after his experience of the Mother was complete and he could share its wonders with others: "When, during the evening service, the temples rang with the sound of bells and conch shells, I would climb to the roof of the *kuthi* [the bungalow] of the garden and, writhing in anguish of heart, cry at the top of my voice 'Come my children! Oh, where are you? I cannot bear to live without you!' A mother never longed so intensely for the sight of her child, nor a friend for his companions, nor a lover for his sweetheart, as I longed for them." Ramakrishna is still crying out to us from the heart of the Mother. On how many of us, and how deeply we respond to him and his example, will depend a good part of our survival.

I would like to dedicate this introduction to
my mother's and my beloved friend, "Bussa,"
Mrs. M. R. Das, for her profound elegance of heart.

Sri Ramakrishna in samadhi *during devotional singing at Keshab Sen's house*
(The Master is supported by his nephew Hriday.)

Preface □

One of the greatest spiritual classics of the twentieth century, *The Gospel of Sri Ramakrishna* is a faithful record of the words and interactions of an extraordinary mystical personality who left no written works of his own. The author, Mahendranath Gupta (who published under the pseudonym "M"), was an intimate follower who kept an eyewitness account of the Master's conversations with visitors, devotees, and disciples during the years 1882–1886. This work was originally composed in the Bengali language under the title *Sri Sri Ramakrishna Kathamrita* ("Nectar of the Blessed Ramakrishna's Talk") and appeared in five volumes published in India between 1897 and 1932.

The standard English translation by Swami Nikhilananda, founder of the Ramakrishna-Vivekananda Center of New York, was published in 1942 under the title *The Gospel of Sri Ramakrishna*. Swami Nikhilananda produced an abridged version as well, also titled *The Gospel of Sri Ramakrishna*, and it is from this shorter version that the selections in this volume have been taken. Page citations to the abridged edition appear in brackets following the selections. To find references for quotations in the annotations, please see "Notes," where citations are keyed by section title and note number.

Most of the foreign terms in the text are in Sanskrit, the ancient language of the Indian scriptures. Words in other Indian languages are noted as such. Diacritical marks for Sanskrit have been omitted, and *sh* has been used instead of *s̆*. An exception is the title *Sri*, where *S* (without an accent) is used instead of *Sh* because it is the conventional spelling in references to Sri Ramakrishna. A few other spelling changes have been made to the original text, to conform to modern American conventions. The chapter headings that appear here are not those of the original text. They were created for this book.

In the annotations, close disciples and devotees of the Master are identified only if there was something that seemed especially important or interesting to say about them; otherwise the reader may assume that the names mentioned in the dialogues are those of devotees or visitors.

I am grateful to Swami Adiswarananda of the Ramakrishna-Vivekananda Center of New York, who kindly served as a consultant on this book, and to Barry Zelikovsky (Swami Vidananda), also of the Ramakrishna-Vivekananda Center of New York (www.ramakrishna.org); and to the following people for their help and insights: Jay Prakash Lakhani and members of the Ramakrishna Yahoo! Group, Bruce Hilliger, Ralph Brockway, and Jonathan Burroughs. Thanks also to Jon Sweeney of SkyLight Paths for the opportunity to work on this book and to my editor, Maura Shaw.

Introduction □

It has been said that one moment in the company of an enlightened master is more valuable than a hundred years of sincere worship. Relatively few people ever get the opportunity to meet a man or woman of the highest realization. Yet so powerful is the influence of these great souls that even a written account of what it is like to be in their presence can impart to us the fragrance of their divine companionship.

The Gospel of Sri Ramakrishna is such an account. Well over a century after his death, Sri Ramakrishna (1836–1886) is still capturing hearts and making them long for the truth of divine life, through this classic record of his encounters with disciples and devotees. Because the full-length book is very long and sometimes daunting for newcomers, this collection of annotated excerpts is offered as an entrée into the world of this unique spiritual personality.

Sri Ramakrishna's ecstatic mystical states, the wisdom and humor of his storytelling, his childlike purity, and his expression of both the masculine and feminine energies of divine love are just a few of the qualities, reflected in this book, that make him so appealing. In particular, he is recognized worldwide for his message that all religions are paths to the truth. Of all the noteworthy spiritual leaders produced by India in the modern era, Sri Ramakrishna seems to have played a special role in heralding the movement toward harmony and tolerance in our time. Although at present the world appears engulfed in religious conflict, the seed of unity planted by Ramakrishna must eventually bear its fruit.

Sri Ramakrishna (*Sri*, pronounced *Shree*, is an honorific title) was born Gadadhar Chatterjee in a remote village of the Bengali-speaking region of eastern India now known as West Bengal. His parents were poor brahmins, the highest-ranking social group in the Hindu caste system, traditionally associated with the occupations of teacher and priest. A sensitive child with talent in devotional singing, acting in religious dramas, and making images of deities, Gadadhar received a simple village education and also learned the formal rituals of worship at a young age. At sixteen he traveled to Calcutta to assist his eldest brother, Ramkumar, in his duties as a priest. Within a few years, they began serving at a large new temple complex in the nearby village of Dakshineshwar, Ramkumar becoming priest of the temple of Kali—the great goddess known as the Divine Mother—while Gadadhar was appointed to one of the smaller shrines. When Ramkumar fell ill and died in 1856, Gadadhar assumed the role of priest to the Divine Mother. From this time, the young man's already fervent inner life began to intensify as he plunged into a quest of desperate spiritual longing that would transform him into the God-intoxicated sage revered as Ramakrishna.

He began to spend long periods in solitary meditation and sometimes neglected his formal duties while he lost himself in singing ecstatically before the temple image of Kali. In her he experienced the all-loving Mother of the Universe, despite her frightening appearance (see illustration on p. 134). A fierce black figure, her hair in wild disarray and her tongue protruding from her mouth, Kali has four arms: one hand holds a bloody sword, another the decapitated head of a demon, and the other two make gestures of blessing and reassurance to her worshipers. She wears a garland of human skulls and a girdle made of severed arms. A symbol of the feminine power that energizes all masculine divinity, she stands on the corpse of her husband, Shiva. To this awesome goddess, bestower of both life and death, blessings and misfortunes, Ramakrishna wept and prayed, begging for a vision of her reality.

When his desperation reached its peak, his prayer was granted, and the Mother revealed herself as the infinite, effulgent Ocean of Bliss—the first of many visions of Divinity he was to experience. In the phase of spiritual intoxication that followed, Ramakrishna's behavior—including such sacrilegious acts as feeding a cat with food meant as an offering to the Goddess—appeared outrageous to some. Others, however, accepted his madness as evidence of his realization, for he now directly saw the presence of the Mother at play in all things.

With the idea that marriage might "cure" him, Ramakrishna was encouraged to wed, and at age twenty-three he was betrothed to a five-year-old girl of his own choosing, named Sarada. According to custom, such a marriage would be consummated when the bride reached puberty, but this was never to occur in the case of Ramakrishna and Sarada. Although she eventually came to live with her husband at Dakshineshwar, it was as his spiritual companion and disciple, and he in turn treated her as a living manifestation of the Divine Mother.

In the meantime, Ramakrishna's inner journey continued to unfold through a series of unusual spiritual experiments. In 1861 he came into contact with the first of several gurus, a woman master of Tantra under whose guidance his divine frenzy was transformed into the joyous attitude of a child delighting in the blissful play created by his Mother. It was this guru who first declared Ramakrishna to be an avatar, a direct manifestation of God in human form. Two of the signs of this status, accepted by religious authorities, were said to be his ability to remain for long periods in a state of divine absorption and the power of granting spiritual awakening through his touch.

Over the next several years, Ramakrishna worshiped the Divine under different names and forms—as the avatars Rama and Krishna, as the formless Brahman of Vedanta philosophy, as the God of Islam, and as Jesus Christ. Through his own inner experiences of the truths taught by various sects and creeds, Ramakrishna became a living embodiment of the essence of all true religion. His life itself was his gospel of unity amid diversity.

In time Sri Ramakrishna began to attract wider public notice, and people flocked to his little room in the temple garden overlooking the Ganges River. At the feet of this humble village priest, who spoke in simple vernacular language, sat scholars of Sanskrit, Western-educated Bengali intellectuals, and wealthy landowners as well as ordinary people. The conversations recounted in *The Gospel of Sri Ramakrishna*—recorded by one of the participants, Mahendranath Gupta (referred to in the text as "M" or Mahendra)—took place among the Master's male devotees and disciples, but he had a devoted group of female followers as well. The streams of visitors were entranced by his homespun parables, his profound spiritual knowledge, and the awe-inspiring accounts of his visions. And now and then, as the Master drifted into the state of divine absorption known as *samadhi,* they simply basked in the beauty of his presence.

Sri Ramakrishna's most beloved disciple, Swami Vivekananda, once posed the question of how we are to recognize a true teacher. The Master gave this answer:

> In the first place, the sun requires no torch to make it visible. We do not light a candle to see the sun. When the sun rises, we instinctively become aware of its rising; and when a teacher of men comes to help us, the soul will instinctively know that it has found the truth. Truth stands on its own evidences; it does not require any other testimony to attest it; it is self-effulgent. It penetrates into the innermost recesses of our nature, and the whole universe stands up and says, "This is the Truth."

That radiant presence is here now, as you turn these pages.

Selections from the Gospel of Sri Ramakrishna

1 A *paramahamsa* is one who has reached the highest state of spiritual consciousness—unity with the Divine. The word literally means "great swan" in Sanskrit. In Hindu mythology the *hamsa* is a sacred bird that represents the ability to discern truth from illusion. From a mixture of milk and water, the swan is said to extract the milk, leaving the water behind. A liberated spirit, the *hamsa* flies beyond the Himalayan peaks but then returns to ordinary life—an apt symbol for Sri Ramakrishna's ability to soar into the transcendent state of divine intoxication and then return to normal consciousness to share with others the truth that he experienced.

Paramahamsa is also a title of honor for the highest type of renunciate, who breaks all ties with ordinary life, abandoning all possessions and signs of social status. Ramakrishna may also be considered a *paramahamsa* in this sense (although he was not formally a monk), owing to his utter indifference to worldly life. He is often called Sri Ramakrishna Paramahamsa.

1 ☐ He Was Talking of God

It was on a Sunday in the spring of 1882, a few days after Sri Ramakrishna's birthday, that M met him the first time. Sri Ramakrishna lived at the Kalibari, the abode of Mother Kali, on the bank of the Ganges at Dakshineshwar.

M, being at leisure on Sundays, had gone with his friend Sidhu to visit several gardens at Baranagore. As they were walking in Prasanna Bannerji's garden, Sidhu said: "There is a charming place on the bank of the Ganges where a paramahamsa[1] lives. Would you like to go there?" M assented and they started immediately for the Dakshineshwar temple garden. They arrived at the main gate at dusk and went straight to Sri Ramakrishna's room. And there they found him seated on a wooden couch, facing the east. With a smile on his face he was talking of God. The room was full of people, all seated on the floor, drinking in his words in deep silence.

(continued on page 5)

2 Shukadeva (or Shuka) is held to be the narrator of the Bhagavata Purana, a medieval sacred text that presents spiritual truths in the form of stories. It contains many touching episodes of the childhood and youth of Lord Krishna, demonstrating the intense love and devotion he inspired in others.

3 Sri Chaitanya (1486–1533) was one of India's great mystics of the path of devotion *(bhakti).* In his ecstatic love for Krishna, he identified with Krishna's sweetheart, Radha, the perfect lover of God. Chaitanya himself is worshiped in the *bhakti* tradition as an incarnation of Radha in union with Krishna. Sri Ramakrishna also experienced this mystical identity with Radha-Krishna. On a man's identification with the feminine, see n. 8, p. 118.

4 Puri, in the state of Orissa in eastern India, is where Chaitanya lived.

5 Hari is an epithet for Vishnu, the all-pervading supreme God in the devotional tradition known as Vaishnavism (see n. 4, p. 50). He is particularly worshiped in the forms of two of his human incarnations, Rama and Krishna. The one Reality that manifested Itself as Rama and Krishna also infused the being of Sri Ramakrishna.

6 *Sandhya* is the daily ritualistic worship performed at home by devout Hindus. Conventional religious ritual is only the first stage of devotion. Once a person has developed intense love and longing for God, there is no longer any need or obligation to perform rituals. But until such ritual observance spontaneously falls away, it is considered a necessary preparation for the spiritual path.

7 Om, consisting of the three sounds *a-u-m,* is considered the supreme mantra, or sacred syllable used for meditation. It possesses divine creative power and serves as an acknowledgment of the supreme Self, Brahman.

M stood there speechless and looked on. It was as if he were standing where all the holy places met and as if Shukadeva[2] himself were speaking the word of God, or as if Sri Chaitanya[3] were singing the name and glories of the Lord in Puri[4] with his devotees.

Sri Ramakrishna said: "When, hearing the name of Hari or Rama[5] once, you shed tears and your hair stands on end, then you may know for certain that you do not have to perform such devotions as the sandhya[6] anymore. Only then will you have the right to renounce rituals; or rather, rituals will drop away of themselves. Then it will be enough if you repeat only the name of Rama or Hari, or even simply Om."[7]

M looked around him with wonder and said to himself: "What a beautiful place! What a charming man! How beautiful his words are! I have no wish to move from this spot." After a few minutes he thought, "Let me see the place first; then I'll come back here and sit down."

(continued on page 7)

8 The *nahabat* was one of two music pavilions—two-storied buildings with domed roofs—one to the north and the other to the south of the Kali temple courtyard.

9 The Dakshineshwar temple compound includes several shrines, bringing together the three major strands of Hindu devotional religion—the Shakta, the Vaishnava, and the Shaiva. Each of these sects worships the supreme personal God under a different name and form. The "temple of Bhavatarini" is a reference to the Kali temple, the main structure of the compound. Bhavatarini is a name for Kali that signifies her role as Savior of the Universe. Devotees of the Goddess are known as Shaktas. To the north stands the Radhakanta temple, containing the images of Krishna and his most beloved female devotee, Radha. As a divine couple, Radha-Krishna—the perfect lover and the Beloved—represent union with God through love. The devotees of Lord Krishna are called Vaishnavas. Along one side of the courtyard of these two temples is the row of Shiva temples. Devotees of Shiva—the great God of renunciation—are called Shaivas.

10 A devotee of Kali, Rani Rasmani was a wealthy widow who sponsored the construction of the Dakshineshwar temple compound. (In India, temples and shrines are not used for congregational worship but are places where offerings are made to the deities. It is common for individuals rather than religious organizations to build temples.) Although nicknamed Rani ("Queen"), she was actually a member of the servant caste.

11 *Sadhu* is a general term for a monk or saintly person who has renounced the world. Some *sadhus*, depending on the sect to which they belong, might also be called *sannyasins*, "renouncers."

As he left the room with Sidhu, he heard the sweet music of the evening service arising in the temple from gongs, bells, drums, and cymbals. He could hear music from the nahabat,[8] too, at the south end of the garden. The sounds traveled over the Ganges, floating away and losing themselves in the distance. A soft spring wind was blowing, laden with the fragrance of flowers; the moon had just appeared. It was as if nature and man together were preparing for the evening worship. M and Sidhu visited the twelve Shiva temples, the Radhakanta temple, and the temple of Bhavatarini.[9] And as M watched the services before the images his heart was filled with joy.

On the way back to Sri Ramakrishna's room, the two friends talked. Sidhu told M that the temple garden had been built by Rani Rasmani.[10] He said that God was worshipped there daily as Kali, Krishna, and Shiva, and that within the gates many sadhus[11] and beggars were fed. When they reached Sri Ramakrishna's door again, they found it shut, and Brinde, the maid, standing outside. M, who had been trained in English manners and would not enter a room unannounced, asked her, "Is the holy man in?" Brinde replied, "Yes, he's in the room."

M: "How long has he lived here?"

BRINDE: "Oh, he has been here a long time."

M: "Does he read many books?"

BRINDE: "Books? Oh, dear no! They're all on his tongue."

M had just finished his studies in college. It amazed him to hear that Sri Ramakrishna read no books.

M: "Perhaps it is time for his evening devotions. May we go into the room? Will you tell him we are eager to see him?"

BRINDE: "Go right in, children. Go in and sit down."

(continued on page 9)

12 The word *Master* in this book is a translation of *Thakur,* a Bengali title of respect for a man held in high spiritual esteem.

13 *Bhava* may be variously translated as a divine attitude, mood, emotion, or state of spiritual rapture. At the same time that Ramakrishna was in this ecstatic mood, he retained his awareness of the outer world, "not in the usual way but as waves within the Cosmic Mind" (Isherwood).

Entering the room, they found Sri Ramakrishna alone, seated on the wooden couch. Incense had just been burnt and all the doors were shut. As he entered, M with folded hands saluted the Master.[12] Then, at the Master's bidding, he and Sidhu sat on the floor. Sri Ramakrishna asked them: "Where do you live? What is your occupation? Why have you come to Baranagore?" M answered the questions, but he noticed that now and then the Master seemed to become absent-minded. Later he learned that this mood is called bhava, ecstasy.[13] It is like the way an angler acts when sitting with his rod: the fish comes and swallows the bait, and the float begins to tremble; the angler is on the alert; he grips the rod and watches the float steadily and eagerly; he will not speak to anyone. Such was the state of Sri Ramakrishna's mind. Later M heard, and himself noticed, that Sri Ramakrishna would often go into this mood after dusk, sometimes becoming totally unconscious of the outer world....

After a little conversation M saluted the Master and took his leave. "Come again," Sri Ramakrishna said.

On his way home M began to wonder: "Who is this serene-looking man who is drawing me back to him? Is it possible for a man to be great without being a scholar? How wonderful it is! I should like to see him again. He himself said, 'Come again.' I shall go tomorrow or the day after."

[119–22]

With a joyful face chant the sweet name of God,
Till, like a wind, it churns the nectar sea;
Drink of that nectar ceaselessly
(Drink it yourself and share it with all).
If ever your heart goes dry, repeat God's name
(If it goes dry in the desert of this world,
Love of God will make it flow again).

Be watchful, that you may never forget to chant
His mighty name: when danger stares in your face,
Pray to your Father Compassionate.
Snap sin's bonds with a shout of joy
(Crying, "To God, to God be the victory!").
Come, let us be mad in the bliss of God,
Fulfilling all our hearts' desires,
And quench our thirst with the yoga of love.

—song sung by Narendra *[176]*

2 □ Keep Holy Company

M's second visit to Sri Ramakrishna took place on the southeast veran-
dah at eight o'clock in the morning. . . .

M (humbly): ". . . How, sir, may I fix my mind on God?"

MASTER: "Repeat God's name and sing His glories, and now and then
visit God's devotees and holy men. The mind cannot dwell on God
if it is immersed day and night in worldliness, in worldly duties and
responsibilities; it is most necessary to go into solitude now and then
and think of God. To fix the mind on God is very difficult, in the
beginning, unless one practices meditation in solitude. When a tree is
young it should be fenced all around; otherwise it may be destroyed
by cattle.

"There are three ways of meditating: think of God while doing
your duties, or meditate on Him in a secluded corner of your house,
or contemplate Him in a wood. And you should always discriminate
between the Real and the unreal: God alone is real, the Eternal
Substance; all else is unreal, that is, impermanent. By discriminating
thus, one should shake off impermanent objects from the mind."

M (humbly): "How ought we to live in the world?"

MASTER: "Do all your duties, but keep your mind on God. Live with
all—with wife and children, father and mother—and serve them.
Treat them as if they were very dear to you, but know in your heart of
hearts that they do not belong to you.

"A maidservant in the house of a rich man performs all the household duties, but her thoughts are fixed on her own home in her native

---

1 "Woman and gold" is a translation of the Bengali *kamini-kanchan*, in which the word *kamini* implies a seductress—it does not mean women in general. Sexual desire and greed or possessiveness were identified by Ramakrishna as the most binding obstacles to spiritual progress in our age, and the colorful Bengali phrase became "his shorthand description for the entire conventional world" (Hixon). Sri Ramakrishna did not mean that women are to "blame" for lust, nor did he teach his male devotees to hate women. On the contrary, he revered women as sacred representatives of the Goddess and taught that a man should treat every woman with the same reverence with which Hindus traditionally regard their own mothers. Swami Nikhilananda notes that when Ramakrishna addressed his female devotees, he warned them against attachment to "man and gold."

village. She brings up her master's children as if they were her own. She even speaks of them as 'my Rama' or 'my Hari.' But in her own mind she knows very well that they do not belong to her at all.

"The tortoise moves about in the water. But can you guess where her thoughts are? There on the bank, where her eggs are lying. Do all your duties in the world, but keep your mind on God.

"If you enter the world without first cultivating love for God, you will be entangled more and more. You will be overwhelmed with its danger, its grief, its sorrows. And the more you think of worldly things, the more you will be attached to them.

"First rub your hands with oil and then break open the jackfruit; otherwise they will be smeared with its sticky milk. First secure the oil of divine love, and then set your hands to the duties of the world.

"But one must go into solitude to attain this divine love. To get butter from milk you must let it set into curd in a secluded spot: if it is too much disturbed, milk won't turn into curd. Next, you must put aside all other duties, sit in a quiet spot, and churn the curd. Only then do you get butter.

"Further, by meditating on God in solitude the mind acquires knowledge, dispassion, and devotion. But the very same mind goes downward if it dwells in the world. In the world one only thinks of 'woman' and 'gold.'[1]

"The world is water and the mind, milk. If you pour milk into water, they become one; you cannot find the pure milk anymore. But turn the milk into curd and churn it into butter. Then, when that butter is placed in water, it will float. So, practice spiritual discipline in solitude and obtain the butter of knowledge and love. Even if you keep the butter in the water of the world, the two will not mix. The butter will float.

"Together with this, you must practice discrimination. 'Woman' and 'gold' are impermanent. God is the only Eternal Substance. What does a man get with money? Food, clothes, and a dwelling place—

2 Contemplating the human body (either one's own or another's) as loathsome is a traditional spiritual technique in the ascetic traditions of India, intended to counteract sensual desire and attachment to the limited, perishable physical form.

3 The faithful and one-pointed love of a "chaste wife" for her husband is an ancient ideal of India. Longing for God should become as natural and spontaneous as the intense attraction that a lover feels toward his or her beloved.

nothing more. You cannot realize God with its help. Therefore money can never be the goal of life. That is the process of discrimination. . . .

"Consider: what is there in money or in a beautiful body? Discriminate and you will find that even the body of the most beautiful woman consists of bones, flesh, fat, and other disagreeable things.[2] Why should a man give up God and direct his attention to such things? Why should he forget God for their sake?"

M: "Is it possible to *see* God?"

MASTER: "Yes, certainly. Living in solitude now and then, repeating God's name and singing His glories, and discriminating between the Real and the unreal—these are the means to employ to see Him."

M: "Under what conditions does one see God?"

MASTER: "Cry to the Lord with an intensely yearning heart and you will certainly see Him. People shed a whole jug of tears for wife and children. They swim in tears for money. But who weeps for God? Cry to Him with a real cry.

"Longing is like the rosy dawn. After the dawn, out comes the sun. Longing is followed by the vision of God.

"God reveals Himself to a devotee who feels drawn to Him by the combined force of these three attractions: the attraction of worldly possessions for the worldly man, the child's attraction for its mother, and the husband's attraction for the chaste wife.[3] If one feels drawn to Him by the combined force of these three attractions, then through it one can attain Him.

"The point is, to love God even as the mother loves her child, the chaste wife her husband, and the worldly man his wealth. Join together these three forces of love, these three powers of attraction, and direct them all to God. Then you will certainly see Him.

"It is necessary to pray to Him with a longing heart. The kitten

4 A helpless kitten, whose mother takes it by the scruff of its neck and places it wherever she wills, represents the devotional attitude of self-surrender to God. Vaishnava theologians contrasted the nature of the kitten with that of the baby monkey, which has to hold on to its mother as she swings through the trees. The baby monkey represents the notion that one must make spiritual efforts to win God's grace.

knows only how to call its mother, crying, 'Mew, mew!' It remains satisfied wherever its mother puts it. And the mother cat puts the kitten sometimes in the kitchen, sometimes on the floor, and sometimes on the bed. When it suffers it cries only, 'Mew, mew!' That's all it knows. But as soon as the mother hears this cry, wherever she may be, she comes to the kitten."4

$[122, 126\text{--}30]$

1 Narendranath (Narendra or Naren for short) Datta (1863–1902) later became world-famous as Swami Vivekananda, his religious name as a monk. Vivekananda founded the Vedanta Society in the West in 1895 and the Ramakrishna Mission in 1897, and organized the Ramakrishna Math (Order), whose monks have spread the teachings of Ramakrishna throughout the world. Ramakrishna loved him dearly and said that he was one of the "ever-free" who had come to the world only to teach others. (See his photograph on p. 24.)

2 The Brahmo Samaj was a liberal reform movement led by Western-educated Bengali intellectuals such as the charismatic Keshab Chandra Sen (1838–1884), who was a frequent visitor to Dakshineshwar. In reaction to the intrusion of British rule and Christian missionaries in India, the Brahmo Samaj wanted to revitalize Hinduism. The organization worked to free Hinduism from rituals and traditions (such as priestly authority), to educate women, and to eradicate caste barriers, untouchability, and child marriage.

3 □ God Is in the Tiger

Sri Ramakrishna was sitting on the small couch. The room was filled with devotees, who had taken advantage of the holiday to come to see the Master. M had not yet become acquainted with any of them; so he took his seat in a corner. The Master smiled as he talked with the devotees.

He addressed his words particularly to a young man of nineteen, named Narendranath,[1] who was a college student and frequented the Brahmo Samaj.[2] His eyes were bright, his words were full of spirit, and he had the look of a lover of God.

M guessed that the conversation was about worldly men, who look down on those who aspire to spiritual things. The Master was talking about the great number of such people in the world and about how to deal with them.

MASTER (to Narendra): "How do you feel about it? Worldly people say all kinds of things about the spiritually minded. But look here. When an elephant moves along the street, any number of curs and other small animals may bark and make a noise; but the elephant doesn't even look back at them. If people speak ill of you, what will you think of them?"

NARENDRA: "I shall think that dogs are barking at me."

MASTER (smiling): "Oh, no! You mustn't go that far, my child! (Laughter.) God dwells in all beings. But you may be intimate only with good people; you must keep away from the evil-minded. God is even in the tiger; but you cannot embrace the tiger on that account. (Laughter.) You may say, 'Why run away from a tiger, which is also a

19

3 The sacrificial fire is a daily ritual of the Vedic tradition (based on the ancient scriptures known as the Vedas) in which offerings are made to the gods by casting symbolic substances into the fire such as *ghee* (clarified butter), aromatic herbs, sandalwood, flower petals, and grains.

4 A *mahut* is the driver and attendant of an elephant.

manifestation of God?' The answer to that is: 'Those who tell you to run away are also manifestations of God; why shouldn't you listen to them?'

"Let me tell you a story. In a forest there lived a holy man who had many disciples. One day he taught them to see God in all beings and therefore to bow low before them all. A disciple went to the forest to gather wood for the sacrificial fire.[3] Suddenly he heard an outcry: 'Get out of the way! A mad elephant is coming!' All but the disciple of the holy man took to their heels. He reasoned that the elephant was also God in another form. Then why should he run away from it? He stood still, bowed before the animal, and began to sing its praises. The mahut[4] of the elephant shouted: 'Run away! Run away!' But the disciple didn't move. The animal seized him with its trunk, cast him to one side, and went on its way. Hurt and bruised, the disciple lay unconscious on the ground. Hearing what had happened, his teacher and his brother disciples came to him and carried him to the hermitage. With the help of some medicine he soon regained consciousness. Someone asked him, 'You knew the elephant was coming; why didn't you leave the place?' 'But,' he said, 'our teacher told us that God Himself has taken all these forms, of animals as well as men. Therefore, thinking it was only the elephant God that was coming, I didn't run away.' At this the teacher said: 'Yes, my child, it is true that the elephant God was coming; but the mahut God forbade you to stay there. Since all are manifestations of God, why didn't you trust the mahut's words? You should have heeded the words of the mahut God.' (Laughter.)

"It is said in the scriptures that water is a form of God. But some water is fit to be used for worship, some water for washing the face, and some only for washing plates or dirty linen. This last sort cannot be used for drinking or for worship. In like manner, God undoubtedly dwells in the hearts of all—holy and unholy, righteous and unrighteous; but a man should not have dealings with the unholy,

5 Swami Vivekananda says, "Avoid evil company, because the scars of old wounds [impressions deposited in the mental body by our thoughts, words, and deeds of past lives] are in you, and evil company is just the thing necessary to call them out. In the same way, we are told that good company will call out the good impressions which are in us but have become latent. There is nothing holier in the world than to keep good company, because the good impressions will then tend to come to the surface."

6 A *brahmachari* (Hindi; Sanskrit, *brahmacharin;* fem., *brahmacharini*) is the student or initiate of a guru. Traditionally the term refers to a religious student who observes celibacy, but literally it means simply one who "walks with Brahman."

7 Mantras are sacred syllables, words, or phrases used for meditation or religious rituals. A disciple's initiation by a guru includes receiving a mantra to be used in meditation. In this story, the *brahmachari* first uses a mantra to protect himself from the venomous snake by immobilizing it. Then he acts as a guru toward the snake and initiates it into spiritual practice by giving it a mantra ("holy word") of its own.

the wicked, the impure. He must not be intimate with them. With some of them he may exchange words, but with others he shouldn't go even that far. He should keep aloof from such people."**5**

A DEVOTEE: "Sir, if a wicked person is about to do harm, or actually does so, should we keep quiet then?"

MASTER: "A man living in society should make a show of anger to protect himself from evil-minded people. But he should not harm anybody in anticipation of harm likely to be done to him.

"Listen to a story. Some cowherd boys used to tend their cows in a meadow where a terrible poisonous snake lived. Everyone was on the alert for fear of it. One day a brahmachari**6** was going along the meadow. The boys ran to him and said: 'Revered sir, please don't go that way. A venomous snake lives over there.' 'What of it, my good children?' said the brahmachari. 'I am not afraid of the snake. I know some mantras.'**7** So saying, he continued on his way along the meadow. But the cowherd boys, being afraid, did not accompany him. In the meantime the snake moved swiftly toward him with upraised hood. As soon as it came near, he recited a mantra, and the snake lay at his feet like an earthworm. The brahmachari said: 'Look here. Why do you go about doing harm? Come, I will teach you a holy word. By repeating it you will learn to love God. In this way you will get rid of your violent nature and ultimately realize Him.' Saying this, he taught the snake a holy word and initiated him into spiritual life. The snake bowed before the teacher and said, 'Revered sir, how shall I practice spiritual discipline?' 'Repeat that sacred word,' said the teacher, 'and do not harm anybody.' As he was about to depart the brahmachari said, 'I shall see you again.'

"Some days passed and the cowherd boys noticed that the snake did not bite. They threw stones at it. Still it showed no anger; it behaved as if it were an earthworm. One day one of the boys came close to it, caught it by the tail, and, whirling it round and round,

Swami Vivekananda

dashed it again and again on the ground and threw it away. The snake vomited blood and became unconscious. It was stunned. It could not move. So, thinking it was dead, the boys went their way.

"Late at night the snake regained consciousness. Slowly and with great difficulty it dragged itself into its hole; its bones were broken and it could scarcely move. Many days passed. The snake became a mere skeleton covered with skin. Now and then, at night, it would come out in search of food. For fear of the boys it would not leave its hole during the daytime. Since receiving the sacred word from the teacher, it had given up injuring others. It lived on dirt, leaves, or the fruit that dropped from the trees.

"About a year later the brahmachari came that way again and asked after the snake. The cowherd boys told him that it was dead. But he couldn't believe them. He knew that the snake would not die before attaining the fruit of the holy word with which it had been initiated. He found his way to the place and, searching here and there, called it by the name he had given it. Hearing the teacher's voice, it came out of its hole and bowed before him with great reverence. 'How are you?' asked the brahmachari. 'I am all right, sir,' replied the snake. 'But,' the teacher asked, 'why are you so thin?' The snake replied: 'Revered sir, you ordered me not to harm anybody. So I have been living only on leaves and fruits. Perhaps that has made me thinner.'

"The snake had become righteous; it could not be angry with anyone. It had totally forgotten that the cowherd boys had almost killed it.

"The brahmachari said: 'It can't be mere want of food that has reduced you to this state. There must be some other reason. Think a little.' Then the snake remembered that the boys had dashed it against the ground. It said: 'Yes, revered sir, now I remember. The boys one day dashed me violently against the ground. They are ignorant, after all. They didn't realize what a great change had come over my mind. How could they know I wouldn't bite or harm anyone?'

8 Narada was a great legendary sage and exemplary lover of God.

9 *Mahatma,* or "great soul," is a term for saintly individuals.

10 The "lotus feet" of God or of a God-realized master is a traditional expression. The lotus symbolizes purity and detachment, for the plant has its roots in the mud, while its floating blossom and leaves remain untouched by water or earth. (Modern science confirms the purity of the lotus leaf, which has a "self-cleaning" microstructure, observed in the 1970s by botanist Wilhelm Barthlott at the University of Bonn.) Similarly, the feet are in contact with the earth, yet they are above everything. The "feet" of God are that aspect of the Divine which fully enters into material existence yet cannot be limited or changed by it. In keeping with this symbolism, touching the feet, bowing down to the feet, or meditating on the feet of a personal form of God is a gesture of worship and surrender.

The brahmachari exclaimed: 'What a shame! You are such a fool! You don't know how to protect yourself. I asked you not to bite, but I didn't forbid you to hiss. Why didn't you scare them by hissing?'

"So you must hiss at wicked people. You must frighten them lest they should do you harm. But never inject your venom into them. One must not injure others.

"In this creation of God there is a variety of things: men, animals, trees, plants. Among the animals some are good, some bad. There are ferocious animals like the tiger. Some trees bear fruits sweet as nectar, and others bear fruit that is poisonous. Likewise, among human beings there are the good and the wicked, the holy and the unholy. There are some who are devoted to God, and others who are attached to the world.

"Men may be divided into four classes: those bound by the fetters of the world, the seekers after liberation, the liberated, and the ever-free.

"Among the ever-free we may count sages like Narada.[8] They live in the world for the good of others, to teach men spiritual truths.

"Those in bondage are sunk in worldliness and forgetful of God. Not even by mistake do they think of God.

"The seekers after liberation want to free themselves from attachment to the world. Some of them succeed and some do not.

"The liberated souls, such as the sadhus and mahatmas,[9] are not entangled in the world, in 'woman' and 'gold.' Their minds are free from worldliness. Besides, they always meditate on the Lotus Feet[10] of God.

"Suppose a net has been cast into a lake to catch fish. Some fish are so clever that they are never caught. They are like the ever-free. But most of the fish are entangled in the net. Some of them try to free themselves from it; they are like those who seek liberation. But not all the fish that struggle succeed. A very few do jump out of the net, making a big splash in the water. Then the fishermen shout, 'Look!

@ "Some think: 'Oh, I am a bound soul. I shall never acquire knowledge and devotion.' But if one receives the guru's grace, one has nothing to fear. Once a tigress attacked a flock of goats. As she sprang on her prey she gave birth to a cub and died. The cub grew up in the company of the goats. The goats ate grass and the cub followed their example. They bleated; the cub bleated too. Gradually it grew to a big tiger. One day another tiger attacked the same flock. It was amazed to see the grass-eating tiger. Running after it, the wild tiger at last seized it, whereupon the grass-eating tiger began to bleat. The wild tiger dragged it to the water and said: 'Look at your face in the water. It is just like mine. Here is a little meat. Eat it.' Saying this, it thrust some meat into its mouth. But the grass-eating tiger would not swallow it and began to bleat again. Gradually, however, it got the taste for blood and came to relish the meat. Then the wild tiger said: 'Now you see there is no difference between you and me. Come away and follow me into the forest.'

"So there can be no fear if the guru's grace falls on you. He will let you know who you are and what your real nature is."

—Sri Ramakrishna *[257–58]*

There goes a big one!' But most of the fish caught in the net cannot escape, nor do they make any effort to get out. On the contrary, they burrow into the mud net and all, and lie there quietly, thinking, 'We need not fear anymore; we are quite safe here.' But the poor things do not know that the fishermen will drag them out with the net. These are like the men bound to the world.

"The bound souls are tied to the world by the fetters of lust and greed. They are bound hand and foot. They think that 'woman' and 'gold' will make them happy and give them security, they do not realize that it will lead them to annihilation. When a man thus bound to the world is about to die, his wife asks, 'You are about to go; but what have you done for me?' Again, such is his attachment to the things of the world that, when he sees the lamp burning brightly, he says: 'Dim the light. Too much oil is burning.' And he is on his deathbed!

"The bound souls never think of God. If they get any leisure, they indulge in idle gossip and foolish talk, or they engage in fruitless work. If you ask one of them the reason, he answers, 'Oh, I cannot keep still; so I am making a fence.' When time hangs heavy on their hands they perhaps start playing cards."

There was deep silence in the room.

[131–37]

1 Brahman is God in the absolute state, beyond imagination and conception. Because Brahman is formless, It is distinguished from the personal forms of God worshiped by the world religions; however, in reality It is inseparable from the personal God, because according to Advaita (Nondualistic) Vedanta philosophy, Brahman is Existence in its entirety, One without a second.

2 *Vidya* is knowledge that leads to liberation from illusion and realization of the one divine Existence (Brahman). *Avidya* is absence of knowledge, or ignorance, which is responsible for the illusion.

3 Is duality—the play of opposites that we experience in life—really a total illusion? The nondualist philosophers of India explain by giving the example of a rope lying on the ground, which is mistaken for a snake. As soon as we realize that what we thought was a snake is actually a rope, the "snake" disappears. In the same way, when one realizes that only the one God (Brahman) exists, the illusory duality disappears. But of course there never really was a snake—or a world of duality—at all.

4 In Western religion we associate God with good. In Vedanta philosophy, however, God, being infinite, cannot be limited to one member of a pair of finite opposites: as an indivisible Unity, Brahman transcends the duality of good and evil. For the individual soul in the relative world, however, good and evil do exist, and so the great spiritual masters of India also teach that good is the way to God. Those who are God-realized are beyond these moral categories; but since they are free from attachment and desire, they commit no evil actions.

4 □ Knowledge of Brahman

MASTER: "Brahman[1] is beyond vidya and avidya,[2] knowledge and ignorance. It is beyond maya, the illusion of duality.

"The world consists of the illusory duality[3] of knowledge and ignorance. It contains knowledge and devotion, and also attachment to 'woman' and 'gold'; righteousness and unrighteousness; good and evil. But Brahman is unattached to these. Good and evil apply to the jiva, the individual soul, as do righteousness and unrighteousness; but Brahman is not at all affected by them.[4]

"One man may read the *Bhagavata* by the light of a lamp, and another may commit a forgery by that very light; but the lamp is unaffected. The sun sheds its light on the wicked as well as on the virtuous.

"You may ask, 'How, then, can one explain misery and sin and unhappiness?' The answer is that these apply only to the jiva. Brahman is unaffected by them. There is poison in a snake; but though others may die if bitten by it, the snake itself is not affected by the poison.

(continued on page 33)

5 The things mentioned—genres of sacred literature and philosophical systems—represent different religious traditions within Hinduism: for example, the Vedantins follow the view of the Vedas, the Vaishnavas follow the Puranas, and the Shaktas follow the Tantras. People debate which of these competing views is the truth, but in a sense even holy books and teachings are "defiled," because the only ultimate truth is the stainless Reality of Brahman, which cannot be written in books or spoken in words. It can only be realized for oneself.

"What Brahman is cannot be described. All things in the world—
the Vedas, the Puranas, the Tantras, the six systems of philosophy[5]—
have been defiled, like food that has been touched by the tongue,
for they have been read or uttered by the tongue. Only one thing has
not been defiled in this way, and that is Brahman. No one has ever
been able to say what Brahman is. . . .

"A man had two sons. The father sent them to a preceptor to learn
the Knowledge of Brahman. After a few years they returned from
their preceptor's house and bowed low before their father. Wanting
to measure the depth of their knowledge of Brahman, he first questioned the older of the two boys. 'My child,' he said, 'you have studied all the scriptures. Now tell me, what is the nature of Brahman?'
The boy began to explain Brahman by reciting various texts from
the Vedas. The father did not say anything. Then he asked the
younger son the same question. But the boy remained silent and
stood with eyes cast down. No word escaped his lips. The father
was pleased and said to him: 'My child, you have understood a little
of Brahman. What It is cannot be expressed in words.'

"Men often think they have understood Brahman fully. Once an
ant went to a hill of sugar. One grain filled its stomach. Taking
another grain in its mouth, it started homeward. On its way, it
thought, 'Next time I shall carry home the whole hill.' That is the way
shallow minds think. They don't know that Brahman is beyond one's
words and thought. However great a man may be, how much can he
know of Brahman? Shukadeva and sages like him may have been big
ants; but even they could carry at the utmost eight or ten grains of
sugar!

"As for what has been said in the Vedas and the Puranas, do you
know what it is like? Suppose a man has seen the ocean, and some-
body asks him, 'Well, what is the ocean like?' The first man opens
his mouth as wide as he can and says: 'What a sight! What tremen-
dous waves and sounds!' The description of Brahman in the sacred

6 | The word *Satchidananda* is composed of the words *sat* (absolute existence or being), *chit* (knowledge or consciousness), and *ananda* (bliss). Satchidananda is another name for Brahman. Although Brahman is without qualities or parts, "Existence-Knowledge-Bliss" is used to describe aspects of Its being. *Ananda,* or bliss, is not a state of mind but a reality beyond all mental phenomena, including the experience of joy.

7 | In *samadhi* (sometimes translated as "trance"), the mind is merged with the Divine, so that there is no longer any separation between the subject (the meditator) and the object (God). When asked once how he felt in *samadhi,* Ramakrishna replied, "I feel like a fish released from a pot into the water of the Ganges."

8 | A doll made of salt entering the ocean is like the limited ego-mind trying to comprehend ultimate Reality. Once it enters fully into that Reality, it simply dissolves and becomes one with the Ocean of Infinite Consciousness.

books is like that. It is said in the Vedas that Brahman is of the nature of Bliss; It is Satchidananda.[6]

"Shuka and other sages stood on the shore of this Ocean of Brahman and saw and touched the water. According to one school of thought they never plunged into it. Those who do cannot come back to the world again.

"In samadhi[7] one attains the Knowledge of Brahman—one realizes Brahman. In that state reasoning stops altogether, and man becomes mute. He has no power to describe the nature of Brahman.

"Once a salt doll went to measure the depth of the ocean. (*All laugh.*) It wanted to tell others how deep the water was. But this it could never do, for no sooner had it got into the water than it melted. Now who was there to speak about the depth?"[8]

(*continued on page 37*)

9 Shankaracharya (c. 788–820), also called Shankara, was one of India's greatest philosopher-saints. His teachings of Advaita Vedanta emphasize the absolute oneness of God (Brahman), who is the only Reality, and the illusoriness of all apparent multiplicity.

10 The ego of an ordinary person is a limited identity bound to an individual name and form. According to Vedanta, this false ego is an illusion; our real identity is Pure Consciousness without an object. When the illusion of the false self is shed, the real Self is realized. Some individuals who realize their true identity may simply merge with that Pure Consciousness. Others, like Shankaracharya, retain a kind of ego in order to act in the world and guide others. Swami Nikhilananda notes: "Following the method of discrimination, the jnani [follower of the path of knowledge], in samadhi, merges his ego in Brahman. Thereafter he may come down to the relative plane with an appearance of individuality, but even then he is always conscious of his identity with Brahman. This apparent ego is called the 'ego of Knowledge.' A bhakta, following the path of love, realizes his eternal relationship with God. He too keeps an appearance of individuality on the relative plane. This ego has none of the characteristics of the worldly ego and is called the 'ego of Devotion.'"

11 A *rishi* is a sage, especially one of the ancient seers who received revelations while in a superconscious state; these revelations were the basis of the Vedas, the holy scriptures of mainstream Hinduism.

A DEVOTEE: "Suppose a man has obtained the Knowledge of Brahman in samadhi. Doesn't he speak anymore?"

MASTER: "Shankaracharya[9] retained the 'ego of Knowledge'[10] in order to teach others. After the vision of Brahman, a man becomes silent. He reasons about It as long as he has not realized It. If you heat butter in a pan on the stove, it makes a sizzling sound as long as the water it contains has not dried up. But when no trace of water is left, the clarified butter makes no sound. If you put an uncooked cake of flour in that butter it sizzles again. But after the cake is cooked all sound stops. Just so, a man established in samadhi comes down to the relative plane of consciousness in order to teach others, and then he talks about God.

"The bee buzzes as long as it is not sitting on a flower. It becomes silent when it begins to sip the honey. But sometimes, intoxicated with the honey, it buzzes again.

"An empty pitcher makes a gurgling sound when it is dipped in water. When it fills up it becomes silent. (All laugh.) But if the water is poured from it into another empty pitcher, then you will hear the sound again.

"The rishis[11] of old attained the Knowledge of Brahman. One cannot have this knowledge so long as there is the slightest trace of worldliness. How hard the rishis labored! Early in the morning they would go away from the hermitage, and would spend the whole day in solitude, meditating on Brahman. At night they would return to the hermitage and eat a little fruit or roots. They kept their minds aloof from the objects of sight, hearing, touch, and other things of a worldly nature. Only thus did they realize Brahman as their own inmost Consciousness.

(continued on page 39)

12 Hindu cosmology views time as a cyclic process. The universe is created and dissolved many times, spanning vast time periods. In a cycle of creation, the world moves gradually through four cycles called *yugas*, during which conditions progressively deteriorate. Humanity is said to be now in the fourth period, the Kali Yuga, a dark age of ignorance and suffering. (It is named after a throw of the dice in gambling, not after the Goddess Kali.) After this degenerate age culminates in dissolution, the world will spring forth anew into a long golden age of enlightenment and happiness, the beginning of a new cycle. The date traditionally assigned to the beginning of the Kali Yuga is about 3000 B.C.E.

13 The path of devotion, or *bhakti yoga*, entails love for a personal God (such as Kali or Shiva); an avatar, or human incarnation of God (such as Krishna or Rama); or a God-realized spiritual master who personifies the ultimate Reality beyond all form.

"But in the Kali Yuga,[12] man, being totally dependent on food for life, cannot altogether shake off the idea that he is the body. In this state of mind, it is not proper for him to say, 'I am He.' When a man does all sorts of worldly things, he should not say, 'I am Brahman.' Those who cannot give up attachment to worldly things and who find no means to shake off the feeling of 'I,' should rather cherish the idea, 'I am God's servant; I am His devotee.' One can also realize God by following the path of devotion.[13]

(continued on page 41)

14 The *jnani* is a seeker who follows the path of knowledge, or *jnana yoga*, the method of nondualist Vedanta. The word *jnana* is linguistically related to the words *gnosis* and *knowledge*. Some translators render *jnana* as "wisdom" or "cognition." It refers to knowledge of the individual self as identical with the Supreme Self, Brahman. *Jnanis* (including the followers of Vedanta) use the powers of reason and discrimination to attain this divine knowledge.

"Not this, not this" *(neti, neti)* refers to the indescribable Brahman: one cannot say what Brahman is; one can only say what It is not. As Pure Consciousness itself, Brahman cannot be equated with any object of perception, experience, or thought. Thus, by a contemplative process of discriminating the real from the illusory, the *jnanis* negate everything that is illusory until they arrive at the ultimate Reality. Lex Hixon defines *neti, neti* as "the sensibility that refuses to identify with any finite pattern, any limited experience whatsoever."

15 The *vijnani,* a fully awakened sage who has attained *vijnana* (understanding or spiritual insight), is aware of both the eternal reality of the formless Brahman and the divine play of manifestation.

16 God with attributes (Saguna Brahman) is the personal God, Lord (Ishvara) of the Universe. God in the absolute state, without attributes (Nirguna Brahman), transcends personal qualities. The *jnani* regards the personal God as an illusory manifestation of the impersonal Absolute, but the *vijnani* sees no distinction between them.

17 Just as holding the note *ni* of the Indian musical scale is physically difficult, so staying in *samadhi* for long periods is difficult and could be physically damaging. For the *vijnani,* the ego maintains the link between the state of *samadhi* and awareness of the physical body and the manifest world. Without this link, one cannot return to bodily awareness. Thus the ego is no longer a limitation for the *vijnani* but is seen as a manifestation of Brahman, to be used as an instrument in living the divine life.

"The jnani gives up his identification with worldly things, discriminating, 'Not this, not this.'[14] Only then can he realize Brahman. It is like reaching the roof of a house by leaving the steps behind, one by one. But the vijnani, who is more intimately acquainted with Brahman, realizes something more.[15] He realizes that the steps are made of the same materials as the roof: bricks, lime, and brick dust. That which is realized intuitively as Brahman, through the eliminating process of 'Not this, not this,' is then found to have become the universe and all its living beings. The vijnani sees that the reality which is nirguna, without attributes, is also saguna, with attributes.[16]

"A man cannot live on the roof a long time. He comes down again. Those who realize Brahman in samadhi come down also and find that it is Brahman that has become the universe and its living beings. In the musical scale there are the notes *sa, re, ga, ma, pa, dha,* and *ni;* but one cannot keep one's voice on *ni* a long time. The ego does not vanish altogether. The man coming down from samadhi perceives that it is Brahman that has become the ego, the universe, and all living beings. This is known as vijnana.[17]

"The path of knowledge leads to Truth, as does the path that combines knowledge and love. The path of love, too, leads to this goal. The way of love is as good as the way of knowledge. All paths ultimately lead to the same Truth. But as long as God keeps the feeling of ego in us, it is easier to follow the path of love.

(continued on page 43)

18 Mount Sumeru (sometimes called Meru) is the mythical mountain that is the sacred center and axis of the world.

19 The *gunas* are the three primary qualities of nature. *Sattva* is variously described as pure being, consciousness, tranquillity, balance, and truth. *Rajas* is the dynamic principle of desire, attachment, change, and activity. *Tamas* is inertia, darkness, and ignorance. All that exists or occurs is a result of the interplay of these three forces, which combine in different ways to produce everything in nature. Even modern science might be said to acknowledge this ancient truth of three forces, in the form of Newton's three laws of motion and the three laws of thermodynamics.

"The vijnani sees that Brahman is immovable and actionless, like Mount Sumeru.[18] This universe consists of the three gunas: sattva, rajas, and tamas.[19] They are in Brahman. But Brahman is unattached.

"The vijnani further sees that what is Brahman is the Bhagavan, the Personal God. He who is beyond the three gunas is the Bhagavan, with His six supernatural powers. Living beings, the universe, mind, intelligence, love, renunciation, knowledge—all these are the manifestations of His power. *(With a laugh)* If an aristocrat has neither house nor property, or if he has been forced to sell them, one doesn't call him an aristocrat anymore. *(All laugh.)* God is endowed with the six supernatural powers. If He were not, who would obey Him? *(All laugh.)*

"Just see how picturesque this universe is! How many things there are! The sun, moon, and stars. And how many varieties of living beings! Big and small, good and bad, strong and weak—some endowed with more power, some with less."

VIDYASAGAR: "Has God endowed some with more power and others with less?"

MASTER: "As the All-pervading Spirit, God exists in all beings, even in the ant. But the manifestations of His power are different in different beings; otherwise, how can one person put ten to flight, while another can't face even one? And why do all people respect you? Have you grown a pair of horns? *(Laughter.)* You have more compassion and learning. Therefore people honor you and come to pay you their respects. Don't you agree with me?"

Vidyasagar smiled.

The Master continued: "There is nothing in mere scholarship. The object of study is to find means of knowing God and realizing Him. A holy man treasured a book. When asked what it contained, he

20 The *Bhagavad Gita* is one of the most popular scriptures of ancient India. In it, Lord Krishna teaches the warrior Arjuna the art of life while seated in their chariot on the battlefield just as fighting is about to begin. One of the important lessons of the *Gita* is the true meaning of renunciation (*tyaga* in Sanskrit), which implies inwardly abandoning the desire for the fruits of action while remaining externally active in the world.

21 Chaitanyadeva is Chaitanya (see n. 3, p. 4). The weeping man was moved to strong devotion simply by hearing the story of Lord Krishna in the *Gita*. In the *bhakti* tradition of Chaitanya, such a capacity for love of God is considered higher than an intellectual understanding of the philosophy taught in the *Gita*.

22 Hanuman was a great monkey devotee of Lord Rama who plays an important role in the epic known as the *Ramayana*. He is venerated as a deity throughout India and symbolizes the perfect servant of God.

opened it and showed that on all the pages were written the words 'Om Rama,' and nothing else.

"What is the significance of the *Gita*?[20] It is what you find by repeating the word ten times. It is then reversed into 'tagi,' which means a person who has renounced everything for God. And the lesson of the *Gita* is: 'O man, renounce everything and seek God alone.' Whether a man is a monk or a householder, he has to shake off all attachment from his mind.

"Chaitanyadeva[21] set out on a pilgrimage to southern India. One day he saw a man reading the *Gita*. Another man, seated at a distance, was listening and weeping. His eyes were swimming in tears. Chaitanyadeva asked him, 'Do you understand all this?' The man said, 'No, revered sir, I don't understand a word of the text.' 'Then why are you crying?' asked Chaitanya. The devotee said: 'As I listen to the book, I see Arjuna's chariot before me. I see Lord Krishna and Arjuna seated in it, talking. I see all this and I weep.'

"Why does a vijnani keep an attitude of love toward God? The answer is that 'I-consciousness' persists. It disappears in the state of samadhi, no doubt, but it comes back. In the case of ordinary people the 'I' never disappears. You may cut down the ashvattha tree, but the next day new sprouts shoot up. (*All laugh.*)

"Even after the attainment of Knowledge this 'I-consciousness' comes up, nobody knows from where. You dream of a tiger. Then you awake. But your heart keeps on palpitating! All our suffering is due to this 'I.'

"Once Rama asked Hanuman,[22] 'How do you look on Me?' Hanuman replied: 'O Rama, as long as I have the feeling of "I," I see that Thou art the whole and I am a part; Thou art the Master and I am Thy servant. But when, O Rama, I have the knowledge of Truth, then I realize that Thou art I, and I am Thou.'

"The relationship of master and servant is the proper one. Since this 'I' must remain, let the rascal be God's servant.

"One should not reason too much; it is enough if one loves the Lotus Feet of the Mother. Too much reasoning throws the mind into confusion. You get clear water if you drink from the surface of a pool. Put your hand deeper and stir the water, and it becomes muddy. Therefore pray to God for devotion."

—Sri Ramakrishna *[236]*

"'I' and 'mine'—these constitute ignorance. 'My house,' 'my wealth,' 'my learning,' 'my possessions'—the attitude that prompts one to say such things comes of ignorance. On the contrary, the attitude born of Knowledge is: 'O God, Thou art the Master, and all these things belong to Thee. House, family, children, attendants, friends, are Thine.'

"One should constantly remember death. Nothing will survive death. We are born into this world to perform certain duties, like the people who come from the countryside to Calcutta on business. If a visitor goes to a rich man's garden, the superintendent says to him, 'This is our garden,' 'This is our lake,' and so forth. But if the superintendent is dismissed for some misdeed, he can't openly carry away even his worthless mango-wood chest. He sends it secretly by the gatekeeper. (*Laughter.*)

"Can one know God through reasoning? Be His servant, surrender yourself to Him, and then pray to Him."

[151–59]

1 A *yogi* (fem., *yogini*) can mean anyone who practices the path of yoga, a system of spiritual disciplines aimed at the goal of union with the Divine. Such a person seeks to be always concentrated on God, who is the inmost Self of all. This state of concentration does not necessarily mean that one cannot be mindful in the present moment. No matter what activity the mind and body may be occupied with, at the back of the mind one can be rooted in remembrance of God.

2 The nondualist meditates on "I am He" (*So'Ham* in Sanskrit), one of the sacred mantras of Advaita Vedanta, in which "He" refers to the nameless, formless Brahman, or Pure Consciousness, which is without gender.

5 □ Worldly Duties

It was almost dusk. The Master and M stood talking alone near the door on the southeast verandah.

MASTER (to M): "The mind of the yogi[1] is always fixed on God, always absorbed in the Self. You can recognize such a man by merely looking at him. His eyes are wide open, with an aimless look, like the eyes of the mother bird hatching her eggs. Her entire mind is fixed on the eggs, and there is a vacant look in her eyes.". . .

As evening came on, the temples were lighted up. Sri Ramakrishna was seated on his small couch, meditating on the Divine Mother. Then he chanted the names of God. Incense was burnt in the room, where an oil lamp had been lighted. Sounds of conch shells and gongs came floating on the air as the evening worship began in the temple of Kali. The light of the moon flooded all the quarters. The Master again spoke to M.

MASTER: "Perform your duties in an unselfish spirit. . . . Always try to perform your duties without desiring any result."

M: "Yes, sir. But may I know if one can realize God while performing one's duties?"

MASTER: "All, without exception, perform work. Even to chant God's name and glories is work, as is the meditation of the Nondualist on 'I am He.'[2] Breathing is also an activity. There is no way of renouncing work altogether. So do your work but surrender the result to God."

M: "Sir, may I make an effort to earn more money?"

3 | The Hindu Vedic tradition divided the ideal religious life into four stages: that of a celibate student *(brahmacharin)* of a guru, or spiritual teacher; a "householder" who is the head of a family; a "forest dweller" who practices meditation in solitude; and an ascetic who totally renounces the settled lifestyle and lives as a wandering mendicant. Once a man's children had grown, he was free to devote himself to the practice of meditation, the third stage. Often his wife would join him in this spiritual life (which now included sexual abstinence).

4 | Vaishnavas are worshipers of the god Vishnu, notably in his incarnations as Rama and Krishna. Theirs is the path of love *(bhakti)*, and their worship includes chanting the names of God, devotional singing, dancing, and daily worship *(puja)* of their chosen deity. In the Hindu Trinity, Vishnu is the Preserver (along with Brahma the Creator and Shiva the Destroyer). He is known by various names, such as Hari and Narayana.

MASTER: "It is permissible to do so to support a religious family. You may try to increase your income, but in an honest way. The goal of life is not the earning of money, but the service of God. Money is not harmful if it is devoted to the service of God."

M: "How long should a man feel obliged to do his duty toward his wife and children?"

MASTER: "As long as they feel pinched for food and clothing. But one need not take the responsibility of a son when he is able to support himself.[3] When the young fledgling learns to pick its own food, its mother pecks it if it comes to her for food."

M: "How long must one do one's duty?"

MASTER: "The blossom drops off when the fruit appears. One doesn't have to do one's duties after attaining God, nor does one feel like doing them then.

"If a drunkard takes too much liquor he cannot retain conscious-ness. If he takes only two or three glasses, he can go on with his work. As you advance nearer and nearer to God, He will reduce your activ-ities little by little. Have no fear.

"Finish the few duties you have in hand, and then you will have peace. When the mistress of the house goes to bathe after finishing her cooking and other household duties, she won't come back, how-ever you may shout after her."

M: "Sir, what is the meaning of the realization of God? What do you mean by God-vision? How does one attain it?"

MASTER: "According to the Vaishnavas,[4] the aspirants and the seers of God may be divided into different classes: the beginners, those strug-gling to see God, the perfected ones, and the supremely perfect. He who has just set foot on the path may be called a beginner. He who has for some time been practicing spiritual disciplines, such as

5 *Japa* is the mental repetition of a mantra or a name of God as a meditation.

"*Japa* means silently repeating God's name in solitude. When you chant His name with single-minded devotion you can see God's form and realize Him. Suppose there is a piece of timber sunk in the water of the Ganges and fastened with a chain to the bank. You proceed link by link, holding to the chain, and you dive into the water and follow the chain. Finally you are able to reach the timber. In the same way, by repeating God's name you become absorbed in Him and finally realize Him."

—Sri Ramakrishna

worship, japa,[5] meditation, and the chanting of God's name and glories, is called a struggling soul. He is a perfected soul who has known from his inner experience that God exists. An analogy is given in Vedanta to explain this. The master of the house is asleep in a dark room. Someone is groping in the darkness to find him. He touches the couch and says, 'No, it is not he.' He touches the window and says, 'No, it is not he.' He touches the door and says, 'No, it is not he.' This is known in Vedanta as the process of 'Neti, neti,' 'Not this, not this.' At last his hand touches the master's body and he exclaims, 'Here he is!' In other words, he is now conscious of the 'existence' of the master. He has found him, but he doesn't yet know him intimately.

"There is yet another type, known as the supremely perfect. It is quite a different thing when one talks to the master intimately, when one knows God very intimately through love and devotion. A perfected soul has undoubtedly attained God, but the supremely perfect has known God very intimately."

M: "When one sees God, does one see Him with these eyes?"

MASTER: "God cannot be seen with these physical eyes. In the course of spiritual discipline one gets a 'love body,' endowed with 'love eyes,' 'love ears,' and so on. One sees God with those 'love eyes.' One hears the voice of God with those 'love ears.'

"But this is not possible without intense love of God. One sees God alone everywhere when one loves Him with great intensity. It is like a person with jaundice, who sees everything yellow. Then one feels, 'I am verily He.'

"One who thinks of God day and night beholds him everywhere. It is like a man's seeing flames on all sides after he has gazed fixedly at one flame for some time."

"But that isn't the real flame," flashed through M's mind.

6 Shivanath was a devotee who was one of the leaders of the Brahmo Samaj.

7 *Maha* means "great," and *maya* is the divine power that causes the illusory world of duality to appear real. Lex Hixon calls *maya* the magical "Mother power that projects and veils." The projection—this universe—has "no absolute existence: it exists only in relation to my mind, and to the mind of everyone else," writes Swami Vivekananda; "it has no unchangeable, immovable, infinite existence. Nor can it be said to have non-existence, since it exists and we have to work in and through it. It is a mixture of existence and non-existence."

Sri Ramakrishna, who could read a man's inmost thought, said: "One doesn't lose consciousness by thinking of Him who is all Spirit, all Consciousness. Shivanath[6] once remarked that too much thinking about God confounds the brain. Thereupon I said to him, 'How can one become unconscious by thinking of Consciousness?'"

M: "Yes, sir, I realize that. It isn't like thinking of an unreal object. How can a man lose his intelligence if he always fixes his mind on Him whose very nature is eternal Intelligence?"

MASTER (*with pleasure*): "It is through God's grace that you have understood that. The doubts of the mind will not disappear without His grace. Doubts do not disappear without Self-realization.

"But one need not fear anything if one has received God's grace. It is rather easy for a child to stumble if he holds his father's hand; but there can be no such fear if the father holds the child's hand. A man does not have to suffer anymore if God, in His grace, removes his doubts and reveals Himself to him. But this grace descends upon him only after he has prayed to God with intense yearning of heart and practiced spiritual discipline. The mother feels compassion for her child when she sees him running about breathlessly. She has been hiding herself; now she appears before the child."

"But why should God make us run about?" thought M.

Immediately Sri Ramakrishna said: "It is His will that we should run about a little. It is great fun. God has created the world in play, as it were. This is called Mahamaya, the Great Illusion.[7] Therefore one must take refuge in the Divine Mother, the Cosmic Power Itself. It is She who has bound us with the shackles of illusion. The realization of God is possible only when those shackles are severed."

[*168–72*]

1 "The Holy Mother" is the name by which Sri Ramakrishna's wife, Sarada Devi, was known among his devotees. Sri Ramakrishna had some years ago asked his wife to stay with his mother in one of the *nahabat*s (music towers) because his divine moods and trances throughout the night kept Sarada anxiously wakeful as she watched over him. (Ramakrishna's mother had died several years before the period described in this passage.) The Holy Mother was not only Ramakrishna's disciple and spiritual companion, but became a spiritual guide in her own right. (See her photograph on page 61.)

6 □ A Feast of Joy

Narendra, M, and Priya were going to spend the night at the temple garden. This pleased the Master highly, especially since Narendra would be with him. The Holy Mother,[1] who was living in the nahabat, had prepared the supper. Surendra bore the greater part of the Master's expenses. The plates were set out on the southeast verandah of the Master's room.

While the devotees were enjoying their meal, Sri Ramakrishna stood by and watched them with intense delight. That night the Master's joy was very great.

After supper the devotees rested on the mat spread on the floor of the Master's room. They began to talk with him. It was indeed a feast of joy. The Master asked Narendra to sing the song beginning with the line: "In Wisdom's firmament the moon of love is rising full."

Narendra sang, and other devotees played the drums and cymbals:

In Wisdom's firmament the moon of love is rising full,
And Love's flood tide, in surging waves, is flowing everywhere.
O Lord, how full of bliss Thou art! Victory unto Thee!

On every side shine devotees, like stars around the moon;
Their Friend, the Lord All-merciful, joyously plays with them.
Behold! the gates of paradise today are open wide.

The soft spring wind of the New Day raises fresh waves of joy;
Gently it carries towards the earth the fragrance of God's Love,
Till all the yogis, drunk with bliss, are lost in ecstasy.

2 Premdas is the poet who wrote the song.

3 Shakti is the divine consort of Lord Shiva, and is synonymous with Kali. (In Vedanta philosophy, Shakti is known as Maya.) She is the creative power or energy of Brahman, while Shiva is passive and contemplative. In contrast to the Western view of the feminine principle as passive, here the feminine is the active force, evolving the universe out of its own being, while Shiva, as Pure Consciousness, does nothing.

When the potential for manifestation is activated, it becomes the divine couple Shiva-Shakti—symbolically comparable to the divine couples Radha-Krishna and Lakshmi-Narayana and the principles of Purusha and Prakriti (see the next note).

Brahman and Shakti are thus inseparable aspects of the same reality: "If you accept one, you must accept the other. It is like fire and its power to burn," in Sri Ramakrishna's words.

Upon the sea of the world unfolds the lotus of the New Day,
And there the Mother sits enshrined, in blissful majesty.
See how the bees are mad with joy, sipping the nectar there.

Behold the Mother's radiant face, which so enchants the heart
And captivates the universe. About Her Lotus Feet
Bands of ecstatic holy men are dancing in delight.

What matchless loveliness is Hers! What infinite content
Pervades the heart when She appears! O brothers, says Premdas,[2]
I humbly beg you, one and all, to sing the Mother's praise.

Sri Ramakrishna sang and danced, and the devotees danced around him.

Shortly before midnight Narendra and the other devotees lay down
on a bed made on the floor of the Master's room.

At dawn some of the devotees were up. They saw the Master, naked
as a child, walking up and down the room repeating the names of the
various gods and goddesses. His voice was sweet as nectar. Now he
would look at the Ganges, now stop in front of the pictures hanging on
the walls and bow down before them, chanting all the while the holy
names in his sweet voice. Now and then he said: "O Mother, Thou art
verily Brahman and Thou art verily Shakti.[3] Thou art Purusha and Thou

(continued on page 61)

4   In Yoga philosophy, Purusha is the eternal Spirit or Self (called Atman in Vedanta), and Prakriti is primordial Nature through which the Self becomes manifest. (See also n. 6 below.)

5   Virat is God as the creator and preserver of the physical universe. Put another way, Virat is the universal Self in manifestation as all the gross forms of the material world.

6   The Samkhya school, one of the six traditional systems of Hindu philosophy, teaches that the universe evolves out of twenty-four cosmic principles. Beginning with the union of the masculine Purusha (Spirit or Consciousness) and the feminine Prakriti (Matter or Nature), the material world emerges, transforming from one principle to another, through the action of the three *gunas* (see n. 19, p. 42). The twenty-four principles are (1) unmanifest, undifferentiated Nature, which is the source of all manifest forms; (2) the intellect, or discriminative faculty *(buddhi);* (3) ego, or "I"-consciousness *(ahamkara);* (4) mind *(manas);* (5–9) five sense organs (ears, eyes, nose, tongue, skin); (10–14) five organs of action (hands, feet, organ of speech, organ of generation, organ of evacuation); (15–19) five subtle elements (sound, form, touch, smell, taste); and (20–24) five gross elements (ether, fire, air, water, earth). All of these principles belong to Prakriti (which is both manifest and unmanifest). As Pure Consciousness, Purusha is inactive and does not enter the evolutionary process.

art Prakriti.[4] Thou art Virat,[5] Thou art the Absolute, and Thou dost manifest Thyself as the Relative. Thou art verily the twenty-four cosmic principles."[6]

[176–78]

Sarada Devi, Sri Ramakrishna's wife, known as the Holy Mother

1 Durga is one of the aspects of the Divine Mother. Temporary clay images of a deity are made in India for various festival celebrations. For the duration of the festival, the clay object is symbolically invested with the spirit of the deity. When the celebration is over, the object is cast into a body of water. Hindus do not worship images or idols. They use the images as a focus for their worship of God.

2 Rakhal Chandra Ghosh later became Swami Brahmananda, one of the monks of the Ramakrishna Order formed after the Master's passing. His friend Baburam Ghosh became Swami Premananda. Bhavanath Chatterji was a devotee who had begun visiting Ramakrishna while still a teenager, despite the objections of his parents, who regarded the Master as a madman.

7 □ "Where Is My Krishna?"

It was the day of Vijaya, the last day of the celebration of the worship of Durga, when the clay image is immersed in the water of a lake or river.[1]

About nine o'clock in the morning M was seated on the floor of the Master's room at Dakshineshwar, near Sri Ramakrishna, who was reclining on the small couch. Rakhal was then living with the Master, and Narendra and Bhavanath visited him frequently. Baburam had seen him only once or twice.[2]

MASTER (TO M): "How are you getting along with your meditation nowadays? What aspect of God appeals to your mind—with form or without form?"

M: "Sir, at present I can't fix my mind on God with form. On the other hand, I can't concentrate steadily on God without form."

MASTER: "Now you see that the mind cannot be fixed, all of a sudden, on the formless aspect of God. It is wise to think of God with form at the beginning.". . .

M sat in silence. After a few minutes he asked the Master: "What does one feel while thinking of God without form? Isn't it possible to describe it?" After some reflection, the Master said, "Do you know what it is like?" He remained silent a moment and then said a few words to M about one's experiences when one realizes God with and without form.

MASTER: "You see, one must practice spiritual discipline to understand this correctly. Suppose there are treasures in a room. If you want to see them and lay hold of them, you must take the trouble to get the key and unlock the door. After that you must take the treasures out.

3 One meaning of Krishna's name is "black" or "dark," hence the blackberries.

@ "Some say that there are ten Divine Incarnations, some twenty-four, while others say that there are innumerable Incarnations. If you see anywhere a special manifestation of God's Power, you may know that God has incarnated Himself there. That is my opinion."

—Sri Ramakrishna *[416]*

But suppose the room is locked, and standing outside the door you merely say to yourself: 'Here I have opened the door. Now I have broken the lock of the chest. Now I have taken out the treasure.' Such brooding near the door will not enable you to achieve anything.

"You must practice discipline.

"The jnanis think of God without form. They don't accept the Divine Incarnation. Praising Sri Krishna, Arjuna said, 'Thou art Brahman Absolute.' Sri Krishna replied, 'Follow Me, and you will know whether or not I am Brahman Absolute.' So saying, Sri Krishna led Arjuna to a certain place and asked him what he saw there. 'I see a huge tree,' said Arjuna, 'and on it I notice fruits hanging like clusters of blackberries.' Then Krishna said to Arjuna, 'Come nearer and you will find that these are not clusters of blackberries, but clusters of innumerable Krishnas like Me, hanging from the tree.'[3] In other words, Divine Incarnations without number appear and disappear on the tree of the Absolute Brahman.

"I accept God with form when I am in the company of people who believe in that ideal, and I also agree with those who believe in the formless God."

M (smiling): "You are as infinite as He of whom we have been talking. Truly, no one can fathom your depths."

MASTER (smiling): "Ah! I see you have found it out. Let me tell you something. One should follow various paths. One should practice each creed for a time.

"There are two classes of yogis. Some roam about visiting various holy places and have not yet found peace of mind. But some, having visited all the sacred places, have quieted their minds. Feeling serene and peaceful, they settle down in one place and no longer move about. In that one place they are happy; they don't feel the need of going to any sacred place. If one of them ever visits a place of pilgrimage, it is only for the purpose of new inspiration.

4 | Mathur Babu ("Mr. Mathur") was Mathur Mohan, the son-in-law of Rani Rasmani, who constructed the Dakshineshwar temples. He managed the property for her and looked after Sri Ramakrishna's needs.

5 | Vrindavan (also known as Brindaban)—located about eighty miles south of Delhi—is the region of India identified as the site where Lord Krishna lived and showered love on his devotees thousands of years ago. Visiting this site sent Ramakrishna into rapture because, as he explained, "If a man loves God, even the slightest thing kindles spiritual feeling in him.... At the sight of a cloud, the peacock's emotion is awakened: he dances, spreading his tail. Radha had the same experience. Just the sight of a cloud recalled Krishna to her mind."

6 | Hriday was a "distant nephew" (what Americans would call a cousin) of Sri Ramakrishna's who assisted his uncle during the period of his spiritual disciplines.

7 | The Kaliyadaman Ghat is the legendary spot where Lord Krishna defeated a monstrous venomous snake that had taken up residence in the Jamuna River, poisoning it. Krishna thus saved Vrindavan from pollution.

8 | The Jamuna (sometimes spelled Jumna or Yamuna) is a holy river, sister to the Ganges, which flows past Lord Krishna's birthplace.

9 | Cows are associated with Krishna because he was chief of the cowherds in his village.

10 | Shyamakunda and Radhakunda are places near Krishna's birthplace of Mathura, associated with the divine love of Krishna and Radha. Mount Govardhan is a sacred mountain that Lord Krishna lifted on his finger to shelter his devotees from a storm. A palanquin is an enclosed conveyance (now obsolete) for one person, borne on poles carried on the shoulders of men.

"One undoubtedly finds inspiration in a holy place. I accompanied Mathur Babu[4] to Vrindavan.[5] Hriday[6] and the ladies of Mathur's family were in our party. No sooner did I see the Kaliyadaman Ghat[7] than a divine emotion surged up within me. I was completely overwhelmed. Hriday used to bathe me there as if I were a small child.

"At dusk, the 'cow-dust hour,' I would walk on the bank of the Jamuna[8] when the cattle returned along the sandy banks from their pastures. At the very sight of those cows the thought of Krishna would be kindled in my mind.[9] I would run along like a madman, crying: 'Oh, where is Krishna? Where is my Krishna?'

"I went to Shyamakunda and Radhakunda in a palanquin and got out to visit the holy Mount Govardhan.[10] At the very sight of the mount I was overpowered with divine emotion and ran to the top. I lost all consciousness of the world around me. The residents of the place helped me to come down. On my way to the sacred pools of Shyamakunda and Radhakunda, when I saw the meadows, the trees, the shrubs, the birds, and the deer, I was overcome with ecstasy. My clothes became wet with tears. I said: 'O Krishna! Everything here I see as it was in the olden days. You alone are absent.' Seated inside the palanquin, I lost all power of speech. Hriday followed the palanquin. He had warned the bearers to be careful about me.

(continued on page 69)

11 Gangamayi, a great saint in her sixties, was a devotee of Krishna and Radha, the cowherding girl *(gopi)* whose love for Krishna was so great that she became immortalized as his eternal feminine counterpart, an object of religious devotion herself. Because of Gangamayi's devotion to Radha, she was regarded as a reincarnation of one of Radha's *gopi* companions. When Ramakrishna assumed the devotional attitude called *madhura bhava* (see n. 8, p. 118), he emanated the feminine energy of devotion. Recognizing this, Gangamayi related to him as one "girlfriend" to another.

12 The Nidhuvan is a sacred grove where Krishna played with the *gopis*.

13 Taking the dust of the Master's feet means touching one's forehead to his feet as a gesture of reverence and surrender.

"Gangamayi[11] became very fond of me in Vrindavan. She was an old woman who lived all alone in a hut near the Nidhuvan.[12] Referring to my spiritual condition and ecstasy, she said, 'He is the very embodiment of Radha.' She addressed me as 'Dulali,' 'Darling.' When with her, I forgot my food and drink, my bath, and all thought of going home. On some days Hriday used to bring food from home and feed me. Gangamayi also served me with food prepared by her own hands.

"Gangamayi used to experience trances. At such times a great crowd would come to see her. One day, in a state of ecstasy, she climbed on Hriday's shoulders.

"I didn't want to leave her and return to Calcutta. Everything was arranged for me to stay with her. I was to eat double-boiled rice and we were to have our beds on either side of the cottage. All the arrangements had been made, when Hriday said: 'You have such a weak stomach. Who will look after you?' 'Why,' said Gangamayi, 'I shall look after him. I'll nurse him.' Hriday was dragging me by one hand and she by the other, when I remembered my mother, who was then living alone here in the nahabat of the temple garden. I found it impossible to stay away from her, and said to Gangamayi, 'No, I must go.' I loved the atmosphere at Vrindavan."

About eleven o'clock the Master took his meal, the offerings from the temple of Kali. After taking his noonday rest he resumed his conversation with the devotees. Every now and then he uttered the holy word "Om" or repeated the sacred names of the deities.

After sunset the evening worship was performed in the temples. Since it was the day of Vijaya, the devotees first saluted the Divine Mother and then took the dust of the Master's feet.[13]

[184–88]

1 The Lakshmi Puja is the worship ceremony for the goddess Lakshmi, the divine consort of Vishnu and the goddess of auspiciousness and prosperity.

2 The *chandni* is a roofed terrace at the Dakshineshwar temple compound, with a *ghat* (steps) leading down to the Ganges River, where the Master used to bathe.

3 The Panchavati was a grove of five sacred trees—banyan, peepal, neem, amalaki, and bel—that Sri Ramakrishna had planted in the temple garden. There he performed his spiritual practices *(sadhana)*, and it became the site of many of his visions.

4 Vijay Krishna Goswami headed a branch of the Brahmo Samaj movement that had broken off from the organization led by Keshab. Once a friend of Keshab's, Vijay was now an opponent, so his participation in this outing arranged by Keshab was awkward. But their being together in the holy presence of the Master while he was in *samadhi* must have had some deep inner significance.

8 □ Play of the Divine Mother

It was Friday, the day of the Lakshmi Puja.[1] Keshab Chandra Sen had arranged a boat trip on the Ganges for Sri Ramakrishna.

About four o'clock in the afternoon the steamboat with Keshab and his Brahmo followers cast anchor in the Ganges alongside the Kali temple at Dakshineshwar. The passengers saw in front of them the bathing ghat and the chandni.[2] To their left, in the temple compound, stood six temples of Shiva, and to their right another group of six Shiva temples. The white steeple of the Kali temple, the treetops of the Panchavati,[3] and the silhouette of pine trees stood high against the blue autumn sky. The gardens between the two nahabats were filled with fragrant flowers, along the bank of the Ganges were rows of flowering plants. The blue sky was reflected in the brown water of the river, the sacred Ganges, associated with the most ancient traditions of Indo-Aryan civilization. The outer world appeared soft and serene, and the hearts of the Brahmo devotees were filled with peace.

Sri Ramakrishna was in his room talking with Vijay and Haralal. Several disciples of Keshab entered. Bowing before the Master, they said to him: "Sir, the steamer has arrived. Keshab Babu has asked us to take you there." A small boat was to carry the Master to the steamer. No sooner had he got into the boat than he lost outer consciousness in samadhi. Vijay[4] was with him.

M was among the passengers. As the boat came alongside the steamer, all rushed to the railing to have a view of Sri Ramakrishna. Keshab became anxious to get him safely on board. With great difficulty the Master was brought back to consciousness of the world and taken to a cabin in the steamer. Still in an abstracted mood, he walked

71

5　Pavhari Baba was a well-known ascetic and yogi who was a contemporary of Sri Ramakrishna's.

6　Elsewhere Sri Ramakrishna says, "Mother, what people call 'man' is only a pillowcase, nothing but a pillowcase. Consciousness is Thine alone."

7　In Yoga philosophy, *atman* can mean either the individual self or the Supreme Self; in Vedanta the individual *atman* is regarded as identical with the supreme Atman. *Bhagavan* means "Lord" and is an epithet or honorific for the personal God among the Vaishnavas.

mechanically, leaning on a devotee for support. Keshab and the others bowed before him, but he was not aware of them. Inside the cabin there were a few chairs and a table. He was made to sit on one of the chairs, Keshab and Vijay occupying two others. Some devotees were also seated, most of them on the floor, while many others had to stand outside. They peered eagerly through the door and windows. Sri Ramakrishna again went into deep samadhi and became totally unconscious of the outer world....

Sri Ramakrishna became conscious of the outside world. Nilmadhav of Ghazipur and a Brahmo devotee were talking about Pavhari Baba.[5] Another Brahmo devotee said to the Master: "Sir, these gentlemen visited Pavhari Baba. He lives in Ghazipur. He is a holy man like yourself." The Master could hardly talk; he only smiled. The devotee continued, "Sir, Pavhari Baba keeps your photograph in his room." Pointing to his body the Master said with a smile, "Just a pillowcase."[6]

The Master continued: "But you should remember that the heart of the devotee is the abode of God. He dwells, no doubt, in all beings, but He especially manifests Himself in the heart of the devotee. A landlord may at one time or another visit all parts of his estate, but people say he is generally to be found in a particular drawing room. The heart of the devotee is God's drawing room.

"He who is called Brahman by the jnanis is known as Atman by the yogis and as Bhagavan by the bhaktas.[7] The same brahmin is called priest, when worshipping in the temple, and cook, when preparing a meal in the kitchen. The jnani, following the path of knowledge, always reasons about the Reality, saying, 'Not this, not this.' Brahman is neither 'this' nor 'that'; It is neither the universe nor its living beings. Reasoning in this way, the mind becomes steady. Finally it disappears and the aspirant goes into samadhi. This is the Knowledge of Brahman. It is the unwavering conviction of the jnani that Brahman alone is real and the world illusory. All these names and forms are

8 This metaphor contrasts two modes of mystical union with God. To *be* sugar is the goal of the *jnani,* the knower of the formless Brahman. It means to be merged in the Absolute without any sense of individual identity—one actually *becomes* God. To *eat* sugar means to be merged in God while at the same time having a sense of relative identity—the *bhakta,* or lover, enjoys ecstatic union through devotion to the personal forms of God (as the Divine Mother or other deities of Hinduism or the world's religions), all of which are aspects of one Reality. Some traditions (including Judaism, Christianity, and Islam) deny the possibility of "becoming sugar," instead emphasizing communion with God (as in Martin Buber's concept of the "I-Thou" relationship). For Ramakrishna, these two modes are not mutually exclusive, although he prefers to "eat sugar." His is the ideal of *vijnana,* complete knowledge in which one sees the manifold universe as a manifestation of the formless Absolute. In *samadhi* he would lose consciousness of the outer world completely; but, he said, "God generally keeps a little trace of ego in me for the enjoyment of divine communion. Enjoyment is possible only when 'I' and 'you' remain."

9 Paramatman (*para,* supreme, plus *atman,* soul or self) is the universal, transcendental Self, as contrasted with the embodied soul (*jivatman*). In nondualist Vedanta, Paramatman, *jivatman,* and Brahman are all identical in reality.

10 The yogic practice of withdrawing the mind from the domination of sense objects is called *pratyahara.* It is achieved by means of one-pointed concentration on the object of meditation.

illusory, like a dream. What Brahman is cannot be described. One cannot even say that Brahman is a Person. This is the opinion of the jnanis, the followers of Vedanta philosophy.

"But the bhaktas accept all the states of consciousness. They take the waking state to be real also. They don't think the world to be illusory, like a dream. They say that the universe is a manifestation of God's power and glory. God has created all these—sky, stars, moon, sun, mountains, ocean, men, animals. They constitute His glory. He is within us, in our hearts. Again, He is outside. The most advanced devotees say that He Himself has become all this—the twenty-four cosmic principles, the universe, and all living beings. The devotee of God wants to eat sugar, and not to become sugar.[8] (All laugh.)

"Do you know how a lover of God feels? His attitude is: 'O God, Thou art the Master, and I am Thy servant. Thou art the Mother, and I am Thy child.' Or again: 'Thou art my Father and Mother. Thou art the Whole, and I am a part.' He doesn't like to say, 'I am Brahman.'

"The yogi seeks to realize the Paramatman, the Supreme Soul.[9] His ideal is the union of the embodied soul and the Supreme Soul. He withdraws his mind from sense objects[10] and tries to concentrate on the Paramatman. Therefore, during the first stage of his spiritual discipline, he retires into solitude and with undivided attention practices meditation in a fixed posture.

"But the Reality is one and the same; the difference is only in name. He who is Brahman is verily Atman, and again, He is the Bhagavan. He is Brahman to the followers of the path of knowledge, Paramatman to the yogis, and Bhagavan to the lovers of God."

The steamer had been going toward Calcutta; but the passengers, with their eyes fixed on the Master and their ears given to his nectar-like words, were oblivious of its motion. Dakshineshwar, with its temples and gardens, was left behind. The paddles of the boat

11 Swami Vivekananda recounted: "I was once travelling in a desert in India. I travelled for over a month and always found the most beautiful landscapes before me, beautiful lakes and all that. One day I was very thirsty and I wanted to have a drink at one of these lakes, but when I approached the lake it vanished. Immediately with a blow came into my brain the idea that this was a mirage, about which I had read all my life; and as I remembered, I smiled at my folly, realizing that for the last month all the beautiful landscapes and lakes I had been seeing had been this mirage, but I could not distinguish them then. The next morning I again began my march. There was the lake and the landscape, but immediately came the idea, 'All this is a mirage.' Once known, it lost its power to delude. So this illusion of the universe will break one day. The whole of this will vanish, melt away. This is realization."

12 At the end of a great cycle, the entire universe dissolves and is reabsorbed into the unmanifest state of primordial Nature—only to issue forth once again in a new cycle of cosmic existence. (See n. 12, p. 38.)

13 The Master perhaps referred to the cuttlefish bone found on the seashore. The popular belief is that it is hardened sea-foam.

churned the waters of the Ganges with a murmuring sound. But the devotees were indifferent to all this. Spellbound, they looked on a great yogi, his face lighted with a divine smile, his countenance radiating love, his eyes sparkling with joy—a man who had renounced all for God and who knew nothing but God. Unceasing words of wisdom flowed from his lips.

MASTER: "The jnanis, who adhere to Nondualistic Vedanta, say that the acts of creation, preservation, and destruction, the universe itself and all its living beings, are the manifestations of Shakti, the Divine Power. If you reason it out, you will realize that all these are as illusory as a dream. Brahman alone is the Reality, and all else is unreal. Even this very Shakti is unsubstantial, like a dream.[11]

"But though you reason all your life, unless you are established in samadhi you cannot go beyond the jurisdiction of Shakti. Even when you say, 'I am meditating,' or 'I am contemplating,' still you are moving in the realm of Shakti, within Its power.

"The Primordial Power is ever at play. She is creating, preserving, and destroying in play, as it were. This Power is called Kali. Kali is verily Brahman, and Brahman is verily Kali. It is one and the same Reality. When we think of It as inactive, that is to say, not engaged in the acts of creation, preservation, and destruction, then we call It Brahman. But when It engages in these activities, then we call It Kali or Shakti. The Reality is one and the same; the difference is in name and form.

"After the destruction of the universe, at the end of a great cycle,[12] the Divine Mother garners the seeds for the next creation. She is like the elderly mistress of a house, who has a hotchpotch-pot in which she keeps different articles for household use. (All laugh.)

"Oh, yes! Housewives have pots like that, where they keep 'seafoam,'[13] blue pills, small bundles of seeds of cucumber, pumpkin, and gourd, and so on. They take them out when they want them. In

@ "Kali is none other than Brahman. That which is called Brahman is really Kali. She is the Primal Energy. When the Energy remains inactive, I call It Brahman, and when It creates, preserves, or destroys, I call It Shakti or Kali. What you call Brahman I call Kali."

—Sri Ramakrishna *[378]*

14   In the Indian game of hide-and-seek, the leader, known as the "granny," bandages the eyes of the players and hides herself. The players are supposed to find her. If any player can touch her, the bandage is removed from his eyes and he is released from the game.

the same way, after the destruction of the universe, my Divine Mother, the Embodiment of Brahman, gathers together the seeds for the next creation. After the creation the Primal Power dwells in the universe itself. She brings forth this phenomenal world and then pervades it. In the Vedas creation is likened to the spider's web. The spider brings the web out of itself and then remains in it. God is the container of the universe and also what is contained in it.

"Is Kali, my Divine Mother, really black? She appears black because She is viewed from a distance; but when intimately known She is no longer so. The sky appears blue at a distance; but look at it close by and you will find that it has no color. The water of the ocean, too, looks blue at a distance, but when you go near and take it in your hand, you find that it is colorless.

"Bondage and liberation are both of Her making. By Her maya worldly people become entangled in 'woman' and 'gold,' and again, through Her grace they attain liberation. She is called the Savior, and the Remover of the bondage that binds one to the world.

"The Divine Mother is always playful and sportive. This universe is Her play. She is self-willed and must always have Her own way. She is full of bliss. She gives freedom to one out of a hundred thousand."

A BRAHMO DEVOTEE: "But, sir, if She likes She can give freedom to all. Why, then, has She kept us bound to the world?"

MASTER: "That is Her will. She wants to continue playing with Her created beings. In a game of hide-and-seek the running about soon stops if in the beginning all the players touch the 'granny.'**14** If all touch her, then how can the game go on? That displeases her. Her pleasure is in continuing the game."

BRAHMO DEVOTEE: "Sir, can't we realize God without complete renunciation?"

(continued on page 81)

⎡ⓔ⎤ "A devotee who can call on God while living a householder's life is a hero indeed. God thinks: 'He who has renounced the world for My sake will surely pray to Me; he must serve Me. Is there anything very remarkable about it? People will cry shame on him if he fails to do so. But he is blessed indeed who prays to Me in the midst of his worldly duties. He is trying to find Me, overcoming a great obstacle— pushing away, as it were, a huge block of stone weighing a ton. Such a man is a real hero.'

"Live in the world like an ant. The world contains a mixture of truth and untruth, sugar and sand. Be an ant and take the sugar.

"Again, the world is a mixture of milk and water, the bliss of God-Consciousness and the pleasure of sense enjoyment. Be a swan and drink the milk, leaving the water aside.

"Live in the world like a waterfowl. The water clings to the bird, but the bird shakes it off. Live in the world like a mudfish. The fish lives in the mud, but its skin is always bright and shiny.

"The world is indeed a mixture of truth and make-believe. Discard the make-believe and take the truth."

—Sri Ramakrishna *[309]*

MASTER (*with a laugh*): "Of course you can! Why should you renounce everything? You are all right as you are, following the middle path.

"Let me tell you the truth: there is nothing wrong in your being in the world. But you must direct your mind toward God; otherwise you will not succeed. Do your duty with one hand and with the other hold to God. After the duty is over, you will hold to God with both hands.

"It is all a question of the mind. Bondage and liberation are of the mind alone. The mind will take the color you dye it with. It is like white clothes just returned from the laundry. If you dip them in red dye, they will be red. If you dip them in blue or green, they will be blue or green. They will take only the color you dip them in, whatever it may be. Haven't you noticed that, if you read a little English, you at once begin to utter English words? Then you put on boots and whistle a tune, and so on. It all goes together. Or if a scholar studies Sanskrit, he will at once rattle off Sanskrit verses. If you are in bad company, then you will talk and think like your companions. On the other hand, when you are in the company of devotees, you will think and talk only of God.

"The mind is everything. A man has his wife on one side and his daughter on the other. He shows his affection to them in different ways. But his mind is one and the same.

"Bondage is of the mind, and freedom is also of the mind. A man is free if he constantly thinks: 'I am a free soul. How can I be bound, whether I live in the world or in the forest? I am a child of God, the King of kings. Who can bind me?' If bitten by a snake, a man may get rid of its venom by saying emphatically, 'There is no poison in me.' In the same way, by repeating with grit and determination, 'I am not bound, I am free,' one really becomes so; one really becomes free.

"Once someone gave me a book of the Christians. I asked him to read it to me. It talked about nothing but sin. (*To Keshab*) Sin is the

15 Vedanta does not agree with the Christian doctrine of human nature as inherently sinful, asserting instead that everyone and everything is divine in essence. Sin is but a temporary, illusory appearance (although the consequences of wrongdoing are unavoidable, owing to the law of cause and effect, or karma). For Hinduism, the essential sin is identification with the false, limited, separate ego. Swami Vivekananda says: "The greatest sin is to think yourself weak. No one is greater; realize you are Brahman. Nothing has power except what you give it. We are beyond the sun, the stars, the universe. Teach the Godhood of man. Deny evil, create none. Stand up and say, I am the master, the master of all."

16 Invoking, singing, chanting, or repeating one's favorite name of God is an important practice in the *bhakti* tradition. A name and the object or form that it signifies are inseparable. Repeated properly, with faith and feeling, God's name therefore has a mysterious power to manifest Divinity and to generate God-consciousness.

17 "Righteousness," "truth," and "religion" are some of the possible translations of *dharma*. Its opposite is *adharma*.

one thing people hear of at your Brahmo Samaj, too. The wretch who constantly says, 'I am bound, I am bound,' only succeeds in being bound. He who says day and night, 'I am a sinner, I am a sinner,' verily becomes a sinner.[15]

"One must have such burning faith in God that one can say: 'What? I have repeated God's name and can sin still cling to me? How can I be a sinner anymore? How can I be in bondage anymore?'

"If a man repeats God's name, his body, mind, and everything becomes pure. Why should one talk only about sin and hell, and such things? Say but once, 'O Lord, I have undoubtedly done wicked things, but I won't repeat them.' And have faith in His name.[16]

"To my Divine Mother I prayed only for pure love. I offered flowers at Her Lotus Feet and prayed: 'Mother, here is Thy virtue, here is Thy vice. Take them both and grant me only pure love for Thee. Here is Thy knowledge, here is Thy ignorance. Take them both and grant me only pure love for Thee. Here is Thy purity, here is Thy impurity. Take them both, Mother, and grant me only pure love for Thee. Here is Thy dharma, here is Thy adharma.[17] Take them both, Mother, and grant me only pure love for Thee.'

"Why shouldn't one be able to realize God in this world? But if one lives in the world, one must go into solitude now and then. It will be of great help to a man if he goes away from his family, lives alone, and weeps for God even for three days. Even if he thinks of God for one day in solitude, when he has the leisure, that too will do him good."

[189–97]

The Dakshineshwar temples seen from the sacred Ganges River

9 □ Dive Deep

MASTER: "Many people visit the temple garden at Dakshineshwar. If I see some among the visitors indifferent to God, I say to them, 'You had better sit over there.' Or sometimes I say, 'Go and see the beautiful buildings.' (*Laughter*)

"Sometimes I find that the devotees of God are accompanied by worthless people. Their companions are immersed in gross worldliness and don't enjoy spiritual talk at all. Since the devotees keep on, for a long time, talking with me about God, the others become restless. Finding it impossible to sit there any longer, they whisper to their devotee friends: 'When shall we be going? How long will you stay here?' The devotees say: 'Wait a bit. We shall go after a little while.' Then the worldly people say in a disgusted tone: 'Well, then, you can talk. We shall wait for you in the boat.' (*All laugh.*)

"Worldly people will never listen to you if you ask them to renounce everything and devote themselves wholeheartedly to God. As worldly people are endowed with sattva, rajas, and tamas, so also is bhakti characterized by the three gunas.

"Do you know what a worldly person endowed with sattva is like? Perhaps his house is in a dilapidated condition here and there. He doesn't care to repair it. The worship hall may be strewn with pigeon droppings and the courtyard covered with moss, but he pays no attention to these things. The furniture of the house may be old; he doesn't think of polishing it and making it look neat. He doesn't care for dress at all; anything is good enough for him. But the man himself is very gentle, quiet, kind, and humble; he doesn't injure anyone.

[1] *Tilak* is a mark on the forehead, made with a substance such as sandalwood paste, ashes, or red turmeric powder, to indicate what religious sect one belongs to.

[2] *Rudraksha* are the dried berries of the tree *Elaeocarpus ganitrus,* used as beads for rosaries (*malas*), especially by devotees of Shiva. Usually there are 108 beads on a strand, for counting mantra recitations. *Rudraksha* are credited with various auspicious and healing powers and the ability to dispel sins.

[3] A *dacoit* is a member of a gang of robbers.

"Again, among the worldly there are people with the traits of rajas. Such a man has a watch and chain, and two or three rings on his fingers. The furniture of his house is all spick and span. On the walls hang portraits of the Queen, the Prince of Wales, and other prominent people; the building is whitewashed and spotlessly clean. His wardrobe is filled with a large assortment of clothes; even the servants have their livery and all that.

"The traits of a worldly man endowed with tamas are sleep, lust, anger, egotism, and the like.

"Similarly, bhakti, devotion, may be sattvic. A devotee who possesses it meditates on God in absolute secret, perhaps inside his mosquito net. Others think he is asleep. Since he is late in getting up, they think perhaps he has not slept well during the night. His love for the body goes only as far as appeasing his hunger, and that also by means of rice and simple greens. There is no elaborate arrangement about his meals, no luxury in clothes, and no display of furniture. Besides, such a devotee never flatters anybody for money.

"An aspirant possessed of rajasic bhakti puts a tilak[1] on his forehead and a necklace of holy rudraksha[2] beads, interspersed with gold ones, around his neck. (All laugh.) At worship he wears a silk cloth. He likes outer display.

"A man endowed with tamasic bhakti has burning faith. Such a devotee literally extorts boons from God, even as a robber falls upon a man and plunders his money. 'Bind! Beat! Kill!'—that is his way, the way of the dacoits."[3]

Saying this, the Master began to sing in a voice sweet with rapturous love, his eyes turned upward:

(continued on page 89)

4 The places named are all pilgrimage sites. Ganga is the Indian name for the river Ganges. The holy city Kashi is also known as Varanasi.

5 It is said (for example, in the *Bhagavad Gita*) that whatever thought the mind holds at the time of death will determine one's future existence. Most auspicious would be to think of God or repeat a divine name while dying.

6 The three holy hours are dawn, noon, and dusk.

7 Madan is the name of the poet who wrote the song.

8 Shiva is often shown with five faces and many arms, a symbol of his omnipotence.

Why should I go to Gaya or Ganga, to Kashi, Kanchi, or
    Prabhas,[4]
So long as I can breathe my last with Kali's name upon my lips?[5]
What need of worship has a man, what need of rituals anymore,
If he repeats the Mother's name during the three holy hours?[6]
Rituals may pursue him close, but they can never overtake him.
Charity, vows, and giving of gifts have no appeal for Madan's[7]
    mind;
The Blissful Mother's Lotus Feet are his prayer and sacrifice.
Who could ever have conceived the power Her holy name
    possesses?
Shiva Himself, the God of gods, sings Her praise with His five
    mouths.[8]

The Master was beside himself with love for the Divine Mother. He
said, "One must take the firm attitude: 'What? I have chanted the
Mother's name. How can I be a sinner anymore? I am Her child, heir
to Her powers and glories.'

"If you can give a spiritual turn to your tamas, you can realize God
with its help. Force your demands on God. He is by no means a
stranger to you. He is indeed your very own.

"Furthermore, you see, the quality of tamas can be used for the
welfare of others. There are three classes of physicians: superior,
mediocre, and inferior. The physician who feels the patient's pulse
and just says to him, 'Take the medicine regularly,' belongs to the
inferior class. He doesn't care to inquire whether or not the patient
has actually taken the medicine. The mediocre physician is he who in
various ways persuades the patient to take the medicine and says to
him sweetly: 'My good man, how will you be cured unless you use the
medicine? Take this medicine. I have prepared it for you myself.' But
he who, finding the patient stubbornly refusing to take the medicine, forces it down his throat, going so far as to put his knee on the

⌐ "It is not good to say that what we ourselves think of God is the only truth and what others think is false; that because we think of God as formless, therefore He is formless and cannot have any form; that because we think of God as having form, therefore He has form and cannot be formless. Can a man really fathom God's nature?

"I see people who talk about religion constantly quarreling with one another. Hindus, Mussalmans, Brahmos, Shaktas, Vaishnavas, Shaivas, all quarrel with one another. They haven't the intelligence to understand that He who is called Krishna is also Shiva and the Primal Shakti, and that it is He, again, who is called Jesus and Allah. 'There is only one Rama and He has a thousand names.' Truth is one; It is only called by different names. All people are seeking the same Truth; the disagreement is due to differences in climate, temperament, and names. Everyone is going toward God. They will all realize Him if they have sincerity and longing of heart."

—Sri Ramakrishna *[299–300]*

patient's chest, is the best physician. This is the manifestation of tamas in the physician. It doesn't injure the patient; on the contrary, it does him good.

"Like the physicians, there are three types of religious teachers. The inferior teacher only gives instruction to the student but makes no inquiries about his progress. The mediocre teacher, for the good of the student, makes repeated efforts to bring the instruction home to him, begs him to assimilate it, and shows his fondness for him in many other ways. But there is a type of teacher who goes to the length of using force when he finds the student persistently unyielding; I call him the best teacher."

A BRAHMO DEVOTEE: "Sir, has God forms or has He none?"

MASTER: "No one can say with finality that God is only 'this' and nothing else. He is formless, and again He has forms. For the bhakta He assumes forms. But He is formless for the jnani, that is, for him who looks on the world as a mere dream. The bhakta feels that he is one entity and the world another. Therefore God reveals Himself to him as a Person. But the jnani—the Vedantist, for instance—always reasons, applying the process of 'Not this, not this.' Through this discrimination he realizes, by inner perception, that the ego and the universe are both illusory, like a dream. Then the jnani realizes Brahman in his own consciousness. He cannot describe what Brahman is.

"Do you know what I mean? Think of Brahman, Existence-Knowledge-Bliss Absolute, as a shoreless ocean. Through the cooling influence, as it were, of the bhakta's love, the water has frozen at places into blocks of ice. In other words, God now and then assumes various forms for His lovers and reveals Himself to them as a Person. But with the rising of the sun of Knowledge, the blocks of ice melt. Then one doesn't feel anymore that God is a Person, nor does one see God's forms. What He is cannot be described. Who will describe

⊡ "I have observed that a man acquires one kind of knowledge about God through reasoning and another kind through meditation; but he acquires a third kind of knowledge about God when God reveals Himself to him, His devotee. If God Himself reveals to His devotee the nature of Divine Incarnation—how He plays in human form—then the devotee doesn't have to reason about the problem or need an explanation. Do you know what it is like? Suppose a man is in a dark room. He goes on rubbing a match against a matchbox and all of a sudden light comes. Likewise, if God gives us this flash of divine light, all our doubts are destroyed. Can one ever know God by mere reasoning?"

—Sri Ramakrishna [377]

Him? He who would do so disappears. He cannot find his 'I' anymore.

"If one analyzes oneself, one doesn't find any such thing as 'I.' Take an onion, for instance. First of all you peel off the red outer skin; then you find thick white skins. Peel these off one after the other and you won't find anything inside.

"In that state a man no longer feels the existence of his ego. And who is there left to seek it? Who can describe how he feels in that state—in his own Pure Consciousness—about the real nature of Brahman?

"There is a sign of Perfect Knowledge. A man becomes silent when It is attained. Then the 'I,' which may be likened to a salt doll, melts in the Ocean of Existence-Knowledge-Bliss Absolute and becomes one with It. Not the slightest trace of distinction is left.

"As long as his self-analysis is not complete, man argues with much ado. But he becomes silent when he completes it. When the empty pitcher has been filled with water, when the water inside the pitcher becomes one with the water of the lake outside, no more sound is heard. Sound comes from the pitcher as long as the pitcher is not filled with water.

"All trouble and botheration come to an end when the 'I' dies. You may indulge in thousands of reasonings, but still the 'I' doesn't disappear. For people like you and me it is good to have the feeling, 'I am a lover of God.'

"The Saguna Brahman is meant for the bhaktas. In other words, a bhakta believes that God has attributes and reveals Himself to men as a Person, assuming forms. It is He who listens to our prayers. The prayers that you utter are directed to Him alone. It doesn't matter whether you accept God with form or not. It is enough to feel that God is a person who listens to our prayers, who creates, preserves, and destroys the universe, and who is endowed with infinite power.

"It is easier to attain God by following the path of devotion."

(continued on page 95)

Sri Ramakrishna was teaching the devotees how to call on the Divine Mother. "I used to pray to Her in this way: 'O Mother! O Blissful One! Reveal Thyself to me. Thou must!' Again, I would say to Her: 'O Lord of the lowly! O Lord of the universe! Surely I am not outside Thy universe. I am bereft of knowledge. I am without discipline. I have no devotion. I know nothing. Thou must be gracious and reveal Thyself to me.'"

—*The Gospel of Sri Ramakrishna [283]*

BRAHMO DEVOTEE: "Sir, is it possible for one to see God? If so, why can't we see Him?"

MASTER: "Yes, He can surely be seen. One can see His forms, and His formless aspects too. How can I explain that to you?"

BRAHMO DEVOTEE: "What are the means by which one can see God?"

MASTER: "Can you weep for Him with intense longing of heart? Men shed a jugful of tears for the sake of their children, for their wives, or for money. But who weeps for God? So long as the child remains engrossed with its toys, the mother looks after her cooking and other household duties. But when the child no longer relishes the toys, it throws them aside and yells for its mother. Then the mother puts the rice pot down from the hearth, runs in haste, and takes the child in her arms."

BRAHMO DEVOTEE: "Sir, why are there so many different opinions about God's nature? Some say that God has form, while others say that He is formless. Again, those who speak of God with form tell us about His different forms. Why all this controversy?"

MASTER: "A devotee thinks of God as he sees Him. In reality there is no confusion about God. God explains all this to the devotee if the devotee only somehow realizes Him. You haven't set your foot in that direction. How can you expect to know all about God?

"Listen to a story. Once a man entered a jungle and saw a small animal on a tree. He came back and told another man that he had seen a creature of a beautiful red color on a certain tree. The second man replied: 'When I went into the jungle, I too saw that animal. But why do you call it red? It is green.' Another man who was present contradicted them both and insisted that it was yellow. Presently others arrived and contended that it was gray, violet, blue, and so forth and so on. At last they started quarreling among themselves. To settle the dispute they all went to the tree. They saw a man sitting under

9 The fifteenth-century North Indian devotional poet Kabir is a famous mystic, revered by both Hindus and Muslims.

10 Shankaracharya says, "Only through God's grace may we obtain those three rarest advantages—human birth, the longing for liberation, and discipleship to an illumined teacher." Only as a human being can one strive for and attain liberation from the seemingly endless round of birth and death in illusion. Thus, Shankaracharya asks, "What greater fool can there be than the man who has obtained this rare human birth together with bodily and mental strength and yet fails, through delusion, to realize his own highest good?"

11 *Brahmajnani* means "knower of Brahman."

12 The planes of consciousness are correlated with centers of subtle energy *(prana)* in the body. See n. 4, p. 174.

it. On being asked, he replied: 'Yes, I live under this tree and I know the animal very well. All your descriptions are true. Sometimes it appears red, sometimes yellow, and at other times blue, violet, gray, and so forth. It is a chameleon. And sometimes it has no color at all. Now it has a color, and now it has none.'

"In like manner, one who constantly thinks of God can know His real nature; he alone knows that God reveals Himself to seekers in various forms and aspects. God has attributes; then again He has none. Only the man who lives under the tree knows that the chameleon can appear in various colors, and he knows, further, that it at times has no color at all. It is the others who suffer from the agony of futile argument.

"Kabir[9] used to say, 'The formless Absolute is my Father, and God with form is my Mother.' God reveals Himself in the form which His devotee loves most. His love for the devotee knows no bounds.

"Yours is the path of bhakti. That is very good; it is an easy path. Who can fully know the infinite God? And what need is there of knowing the Infinite? Having attained this rare human birth,[10] my supreme need is to develop love for God's Lotus Feet.

"If a jug of water is enough to remove my thirst, why should I measure the quantity of water in a lake? Suppose a man gets drunk on half a bottle of wine: what is the use of his calculating the quantity of wine in the tavern? What need is there of knowing the Infinite?

"The various states of the Brahmajnani's[11] mind are described in the Vedas. The path of knowledge is extremely difficult. One cannot obtain jnana if one has the least trace of worldliness and the slightest attachment to 'woman' and 'gold.' This is not the path for the Kali Yuga.

"The Vedas speak of seven planes where the mind can dwell. When the mind is immersed in worldliness it dwells in the three lower planes—at the navel, the organ of generation, and the organ of evacuation.[12] In that state the mind loses all its higher visions—it

@ "The spinal column is said to contain two nerve-currents, called *ida* and *pingala*. (These have been identified, I do not know how correctly, with the sensory and motor nerves of our Western physiology.) Ida is said to be on the left of the spinal column; pingala on the right. In the middle is a passage which is called the *sushumna*. When the kundalini is aroused, it passes up the sushumna; which otherwise, in the case of normally unspiritual people, remains closed. When Ramakrishna speaks of the centres of the navel, heart, throat, etc., he is using physical organs to indicate the approximate positions of these centres; actually, they are located within the sushumna itself.

"These centres are also often called 'lotuses' in Hindu writings on the subject, because they are said to appear in the form of a lotus to those whose spiritual vision enables them to see them. It is wrong to think of the centres as being gross physical organs; but it must be remembered, on the other hand, that Hindu physiology makes no sharp distinction between gross and subtle. It is all a question of degree.

"It was noticed that, in the case of Ramakrishna, the ascent of the kundalini was accompanied by a constant and powerful movement of the blood towards the chest and brain. In consequence of this, the skin of his chest was always flushed."

—Christopher Isherwood

broods only on 'woman' and 'gold.' The fourth plane of the mind is at the heart. When the mind dwells there, one has the first glimpse of spiritual consciousness. One sees light all around. Such a man, perceiving the divine light, becomes speechless with wonder and says: 'Ah! What is this? What is this?' His mind does not go downward to the objects of the world.

"The fifth plane of the mind is at the throat. When the mind reaches this, the aspirant becomes free from all ignorance and illusion. He does not enjoy talking or hearing about anything but God. If people talk about worldly things he leaves the place at once.

"The sixth plane is at the forehead. When the mind dwells there, the aspirant sees the form of God day and night. But even then a little trace of ego remains. At the sight of that incomparable beauty of God's form, one becomes intoxicated and rushes forth to touch and embrace it. But one doesn't succeed. It is like the light inside a lantern. One feels as if one could touch the light, but one cannot on account of the glass.

"In the top of the head is the seventh plane. When the mind rises there, one goes into samadhi. Then the Brahmajnani directly perceives Brahman. But in that state his body does not last many days. He remains unconscious of the outer world. If milk is poured into his mouth, it runs out. Dwelling on this plane of consciousness, he gives up his body in twenty-one days. That is the condition of the Brahmajnani. But yours is the path of devotion. That is a very good and easy path.

"Once a man said to me, 'Sir, can you teach me quickly the thing you call samadhi?' (All laugh.)

"After a man has attained samadhi, all his actions drop away. All devotional activities, such as worship, japa, and the like, as well as all worldly duties, cease to exist for such a person. At the beginning there is much ado about work. As a man makes progress toward God, the outer display of his work diminishes, so much so that he cannot

[e] "What will you gain by floating on the surface? Dive a little under the water. The gems lie deep under the water; so what is the good of throwing your arms and legs about on the surface? A real gem is heavy. It doesn't float; it sinks to the bottom. To get the real gem you must dive deep."

—Sri Ramakrishna *[368–69]*

even sing God's name and glories. *(To Shivanath)* As long as you were not here at the meeting, people talked a great deal about you and your virtues. But no sooner had you arrived here than all that stopped. Now the very sight of you makes everyone happy. They now simply say, 'Ah! Here is Shivanath Babu.' All other talk about you has stopped.

"Therefore I say, at the beginning of religious life a man makes much ado about work, but as his mind dives deeper into God he becomes less active. Last of all comes the renunciation of work, followed by samadhi.

"Generally the body does not remain alive after the attainment of samadhi. The only exceptions are sages like Narada, who live in order to bring spiritual light to others; the same thing is true of Divine Incarnations, like Chaitanya. After the well is dug one generally throws away the spade and the basket. But some keep them in order to help their neighbors. The great souls who retain their bodies after samadhi feel compassion for the suffering of others. They are not so selfish as to be satisfied with their own illumination.

(To Shivanath and the other Brahmo devotees) "Can you tell me why you dwell so much on the powers and glories of God? I asked the same thing of Keshab Sen. One day Keshab and his party came to the temple garden at Dakshineshwar. I wanted to hear how they lectured. A meeting was arranged in the paved courtyard above the bathing ghat on the Ganges, where Keshab gave a talk. He spoke very well. I went into a trance. After the lecture I said to Keshab: 'Why do you so often say such things as: "O God, what beautiful flowers Thou hast made! O God, Thou hast created the heavens, the stars, and the ocean!" and so on?' Those who love splendor themselves are fond of dwelling on God's splendor.

"Once a thief stole the jewels from the images in the temple of Radhakanta. Mathur Babu entered the temple and said to the Deity: 'What a shame, O God! You couldn't save Your own ornaments.' 'The

13 "He who has Lakshmi for His handmaid" is Vishnu, to whom the Radhakanta temple is dedicated. Since Lakshmi, the consort of Vishnu, is the very embodiment of riches, he would have no need of mere jewelry. Similarly, God has no need of our praise. It is enough if we love Him.

14 Ramakrishna loved Narendra (Swami Vivekananda) to an extraordinary degree. He recognized him as an incarnation of one of his "eternal companions."

idea!' I said to Mathur. 'Does He who has Lakshmi, the Goddess of Wealth, for His handmaid and attendant ever lack any splendor?[13] Those jewels may be precious to you, but to God they are no better than lumps of clay. Shame on you! You shouldn't have spoken so meanly. What riches can you give to God to magnify His glory?'

"Therefore I say, a man seeks the person in whom he finds joy. What need has he to ask where that person lives, or the number of his houses, gardens, relatives, and servants, or the amount of his wealth? I forget everything when I see Narendra.[14]

"Dive deep in the sweetness of God's Bliss. What need have we of His infinite creation and unlimited glory?"

The Master sang:

Dive deep, O mind, dive deep in the Ocean of God's beauty;
If you can plunge to the uttermost depths,
There you will find the gem of Love.

Seek out, O mind, seek out and find Vrindavan in your heart.

Light up, O mind, light up true wisdom's shining lamp,
And it will burn with a steady flame
Unceasingly within your heart.

[204–15]

@ "Worldly people will never listen to you if you ask them to renounce everything and devote themselves wholeheartedly to God. Therefore Chaitanya and Nitai [his disciple], after some deliberation, made an arrangement to attract the worldly. They would say to such persons, 'Come, repeat the name of Hari, and you shall have a delicious soup of magur fish and the embrace of a young woman.' Many people, attracted by the fish and the woman, would chant the name of God. After tasting a little of the nectar of God's hallowed name, they would soon realize that the 'fish soup' really meant the tears they shed for love of God, while the 'young woman' signified the earth. The embrace of the woman meant rolling on the ground in the rapture of divine love."

—Sri Ramakrishna

10 □ The Spirit of Renunciation

Sri Ramakrishna began to describe worldly people.

MASTER: "Bound creatures, entangled in worldliness, will not come to their senses at all. They suffer so much misery and agony, they face so many dangers, and yet they will not wake up.

"The camel loves to eat thorny bushes. The more it eats the thorns, the more the blood gushes from its mouth. Still it must eat thorny plants and will not give them up. The man of worldly nature suffers so much sorrow and affliction, but he forgets it all in a few days and begins his old life over again. Suppose a man has lost his wife or she has turned unfaithful. Lo! He marries again.

"Or take the instance of a mother: her son dies and she feels bitter grief; but after a few days she forgets all about it. The mother, so overwhelmed with sorrow a few days before, now attends to her toilet and puts on her jewelry. A father becomes bankrupt through the marriage of his daughters, yet he goes on having children year after year. People are ruined by litigation, yet they go to court all the same. There are men who cannot feed the children they have, who cannot clothe them or provide decent shelter for them; yet they have more children every year.

"Again, the worldly man is like a snake trying to swallow a mole. The snake can neither swallow the mole nor give it up. The bound soul may have realized that there is no substance to the world—that the world is like a hog plum, only stone and skin—but still he cannot give it up and turn his mind to God.

(continued on page 107)

1 This is the attitude appropriate for a renouncer. For a householder, as Ramakrishna stated earlier, it is appropriate to love and serve one's family "but know in your heart of hearts that they do not belong to you."

"I once met a relative of Keshab Sen, fifty years old. He was playing cards. As if the time had not yet come for him to think of God!

"There is another characteristic of the bound soul. If you remove
him from his worldly surroundings to a spiritual environment, he
will pine away. The worm that grows in filth feels very happy there.
It thrives in filth. It will die if you put it in a pot of rice."

All remained silent.

VIJAY: "What must the bound soul's condition of mind be in order to
achieve liberation?"

MASTER: "He can free himself from attachment to 'woman' and 'gold' if,
by the grace of God, he cultivates a spirit of strong renunciation.
What is this strong renunciation? One who has only a mild spirit of
renunciation says, 'Well, all will happen in the course of time; let me
now simply repeat God's name.' But a man possessed of a strong spirit
of renunciation feels restless for God, as a mother feels for her child.
A man of strong renunciation seeks nothing but God. He regards
the world as a deep well and feels as if he were going to be drowned
in it. He looks on his relatives as venomous snakes;[1] he wants to fly
away from them. And he goes away too. He never says to himself,
'Let me first make some arrangement for my family and then I shall
think of God.' He has great inward resolution.

"Let me tell you a story about strong renunciation. At one time
there was a drought in a certain part of the country. The farmers
began to cut long channels to bring water to their fields. One farmer
was a man of stubborn determination. He took a vow that he would
not stop digging until the channel connected his field with the river.
He set to work. The time came for his bath, and his wife sent their
daughter to him with oil. 'Father,' said the girl, 'it is already late. Rub
your body with oil and take your bath.' 'Go away!' thundered the
farmer. 'I have too much to do now.' It was past midday and the
farmer was still at work in his field. He didn't even think of his bath.

"You should renounce mentally. Live the life of a householder in a spirit of detachment. Where will you go away from the world? Live in the world like a cast-off leaf in a gale. Such a leaf is sometimes blown inside a house and sometimes to a rubbish heap. The leaf goes wherever the wind blows it—sometimes to a good place and sometimes to a bad. Now God has put you in the world. That is good. Stay here. Again, when He lifts you from here and puts you in a better place, there will be time enough to think about what to do then.

"God has put you in the world. What can you do about it? Resign everything to Him. Surrender yourself at His feet. Then there will be no more confusion. Then you will realize that it is God who does everything."

—Sri Ramakrishna *[353–54]*

Then his wife came and said: 'Why haven't you taken your bath? The food is getting cold. You overdo everything. You can finish the rest tomorrow or even today after dinner.' The farmer scolded her furiously and ran at her, spade in hand, crying: 'What? Have you no sense? There's no rain. The crops are dying. What will the children eat? You'll all starve to death. I have taken a vow not to think of bath and food today before I bring water to my field.' The wife saw his state of mind and ran away in fear. Through a whole day's back-breaking labor the farmer managed by evening to connect his field with the river. Then he sat down and watched the water flowing into the field with a murmuring sound. His mind was filled with peace and joy. He went home, called his wife, and said to her, 'Now give me some oil and prepare me a smoke.' With serene mind he finished his bath and meal, retired to bed, and snored to his heart's content. The determination he showed is an example of strong renunciation.

"Now, there was another farmer who was also digging a channel to bring water to his field. His wife, too, came to the field and said to him: 'It's very late. Come home. It isn't necessary to overdo things.' The farmer didn't protest much, but put aside his spade and said to his wife, 'Well, I'll go home since you ask me to.' (*All laugh.*) That man never succeeded in irrigating his field. This is a case of mild renunciation.

"As without strong determination the farmer cannot bring water to his field, so also without intense yearning, a man cannot realize God."

[221–24]

1 Maya creates the illusory sense of being a separate individual ego.

2 *Mukti*, or liberation, is the goal of life. It means shedding the illusion of the false ego and permanently realizing one's identity with Brahman. In the nondualistic schools of Hinduism, a *jivanmukta* is defined as one who has attained this state while still embodied. In other schools, liberation is seen as occurring upon the death of the body. The *jivanmukta* is both immersed in God-consciousness and aware of phenomenal existence. The lifestyles of various *jivanmuktas* vary, some being active in the world, others withdrawing into divine bliss. In either case, the very presence of the person is a source of blessing to others, even if he or she has no duty to guide spiritual seekers.

3 *Brahmajnana* is the knowledge of Brahman.

11 □ "I Am the Servant of God"

VIJAY: "Sir, why are we bound like this? Why don't we see God?"

MASTER: "Maya is nothing but the egotism of the embodied soul.[1] This egotism has covered everything like a veil. All troubles come to an end when the ego dies. If by God's grace a man but once realizes that he is not the doer, then he at once becomes a jivanmukta:[2] though living in the body, he is liberated. He has nothing else to fear.

"This maya, that is to say, the ego, is like a cloud. The sun cannot be seen on account of a thin patch of cloud; when that disappears one sees the sun. If by the guru's grace one's ego vanishes, then one sees God. . . .

VIJAY: "If without destroying the 'I' a man cannot get rid of attachment to the world and consequently cannot experience samadhi, then it would be wise for him to follow the path of Brahmajnana[3] to attain samadhi. If the 'I' persists in the path of devotion, then one should rather choose the path of knowledge."

MASTER: "It is true that one or two can get rid of the 'I' through samadhi; but these cases are very rare. You may indulge in thousands of reasonings, but still the 'I' comes back. You may cut the peepal tree to the very root today, but you will notice a sprout springing up tomorrow. Therefore if the 'I' must remain, let the rascal remain as the 'servant I.' As long as you live, you should say, 'O God, Thou art the Master and I am Thy servant.' The 'I' that feels, 'I am the servant of God, I am His devotee' does not injure one."

(continued on page 113)

4 The legendary philosopher's stone is a substance that changes base metal into gold. The real philosopher's stone is the grace of a God-realized master, who imparts spiritual awakening through a touch, a glance, or other means, and who can raise even an ordinary person to the highest level of consciousness (symbolized by gold).

5 An *anna* is a coin of low denomination, comparable to a penny.

6 Sri Ramakrishna says, "Lovers of God do not belong to any caste." Such social conventions simply fall away from one who has realized God. Ramakrishna himself ignored the formal rules of caste separation and ritual purity usually observed by brahmins.

VIJAY *(to the Master)*: "Sir, you ask us to renounce the 'wicked I.' Is there any harm in the 'servant I'?"

MASTER: "The 'servant I'—that is, the feeling, 'I am the servant of God, I am the devotee of God'—does not injure one. On the contrary, it helps one realize God."

VIJAY: "Well, sir, what becomes of the lust, anger, and other passions of one who keeps the 'servant I'?"

MASTER: "If a man truly feels like that, then he has only the semblance of lust, anger, and the like. If, after attaining God, he looks on himself as the servant or the devotee of God, then he cannot injure anyone. By touching the philosopher's stone[4] a sword is turned into gold. It keeps the appearance of a sword but cannot injure.

"When the dry branch of a coconut palm drops to the ground, it leaves only a mark on the trunk indicating that once there was a branch at that place. In like manner, he who has attained God keeps only an appearance of ego; there remains in him only a semblance of anger and lust. He becomes like a child. A child has no attachment to the three gunas—sattva, rajas, and tamas. He becomes as quickly detached from a thing as he becomes attached to it. You can cajole him out of a cloth worth five rupees with a doll worth an anna,[5] though at first he may say with great determination: 'No, I won't give it to you. My daddy brought it for me.' Again, all persons are the same to a child. He has no feeling of high and low in regard to persons. So he doesn't discriminate about caste.[6] The child doesn't know hate or what is holy or unholy.

"Even after attaining samadhi some retain the 'servant ego' or the 'devotee ego.' The bhakta keeps this 'I-consciousness.' He says, 'O God, Thou art the Master and I am Thy servant; Thou art the Lord and I am Thy devotee.' He feels that way even after the realization of God. His 'I' is not completely effaced. Again, by constantly practicing this kind of 'I-consciousness,' one ultimately attains God. This is called bhakti yoga.

@ "In the Kali Yuga one does not hear God's voice, it is said, except through the mouth of a child or a madman or some such person."

—Sri Ramakrishna *[351]*

"One can attain the Knowledge of Brahman, too, by following the path of bhakti. God is all-powerful. He may give His devotee Brahmajnana also, if He so wills. But the devotee generally doesn't seek the Knowledge of the Absolute. He would rather have the consciousness that God is the Master and he the servant, or that God is the Divine Mother and he the child."

VIJAY: "But those who discriminate according to the Vedanta philosophy also realize Him in the end, don't they?"

MASTER: "Yes, one may reach Him by following the path of discrimination too: that is called jnana yoga. But it is an extremely difficult path. If a man acquires the firm knowledge that Brahman alone is real and the world illusory, then his mind merges in samadhi. But, as I told you, in the Kali Yuga the life of a man depends entirely on food. How can he have the consciousness that Brahman alone is real and the world illusory? In the Kali Yuga it is difficult to have the feeling, 'I am not the body, I am not the mind, I am not the twenty-four cosmic principles; I am beyond pleasure and pain, I am above disease and grief, old age and death.' However you may reason and argue, the feeling that the body is identical with the soul will somehow crop up from an unexpected quarter. One cannot get rid of this identification with the body; therefore the path of bhakti is best for the people of the Kali Yuga. It is an easy path.

"And there is the saying: 'I don't want to become sugar; I want to eat it.' I never feel like saying, 'I am Brahman.' I say, 'Thou art my Lord and I am Thy servant.' My desire is to sing God's name and glories. It is very good to look on God as the Master and on oneself as His servant. Further, you see, people speak of the waves as belonging to the Ganges; but no one says that the Ganges belongs to the waves. The feeling 'I am He' is not wholesome. A man who entertains such an idea, while looking on his body as the Self, causes himself great harm. He cannot go forward in spiritual life; he drags himself down.

7 *Prema-bhakti* is loving devotion, also known as *parabhakti*, or supreme love for God. *Raga-bhakti* is passionate attachment to God.

As a divine couple, Radha-Krishna—the perfect lover and the Beloved—represent union with God through love

He deceives himself as well as others. He cannot understand his own state of mind.

"But it isn't any and every kind of bhakti that enables one to realize God. One cannot realize God without prema-bhakti. Another name for prema-bhakti is raga-bhakti.[7] God cannot be realized without love and longing. Unless one has learned to love God, one cannot realize Him.

"There is another kind of bhakti, known as vaidhi-bhakti, according to which one must repeat God's name a fixed number of times, fast, make pilgrimages laid down in the scriptures, worship God with prescribed offerings, make a number of sacrifices, and so forth and so on. By continuing such practices a long time, one gradually acquires raga-bhakti. God cannot be realized until one has raga-bhakti. One must love God. In order to realize God, one must be completely free from worldliness and direct all of one's mind to Him.

"But some acquire raga-bhakti directly. It is innate in them. They have it from their very childhood. Even at an early age they weep for God. Vaidhi-bhakti is like moving a fan to make a breeze. One needs the fan to make the breeze. Similarly, one practices japa, austerity, and fasting, in order to acquire love of God. But the fan is set aside when the southern breeze blows of itself. Such actions as japa and austerity drop away when one spontaneously feels love of God. Who, indeed, will perform the ceremonies enjoined in the scriptures, when mad with love of God?

"Devotion to God may be said to be 'green' so long as it doesn't grow into love of God; but it becomes 'ripe' when it has grown into such love.

"A man with 'green' bhakti cannot assimilate spiritual talk and instruction; but one with 'ripe' bhakti can. The image that falls on a photographic plate covered with black film [silver nitrate] is retained. On the other hand, thousands of images may be reflected on a bare piece of glass, but not one of them is retained. As the object moves

8 | Traditionally in *bhakti,* there are several devotional attitudes (*bhavas*) that may be adopted in relationship to the personal God. One may take the attitude of a worshiper toward the worshiped. One may love God as a child loves its mother or father, or as a devoted servant loves the master. The devotee may relate to God as one friend to another, or as the parent of a Divine Child. And finally, one may approach God as a wife loves her husband or the lover adores the beloved.

Ramakrishna primarily experienced himself as a child of the Divine Mother, but at various times he entered other moods. On occasion he took on the state of "handmaid" to the Mother, performing worship while wearing women's clothing and jewelry (so authentic was his feminine attitude that even his close relatives did not recognize him). By playing the part of Hanuman, the legendary monkey god who served Rama, he became the ideal servant of God. He also felt the sweet love of a mother for the divine child Rama. And in the approach to God as a lover—the *madhura bhava,* or sweet mood—he would identify with Radha, the sweetheart of Lord Krishna, or with Sita, who even forgot her own body in the intensity of her devotion to her husband, Lord Rama.

Swami Nikhilananda comments that while practicing this mood of *madhura bhava,* "the male devotee often regards himself as a woman, in order to develop the most intense form of love for Sri Krishna, the only Purusha, or man, in the universe. This assumption of the attitude of the opposite sex has deep psychological significance. It is a matter of common experience that an idea may be cultivated to such an intense degree that every idea alien to it is driven from the mind. This peculiarity of the mind may be utilized for the subjugation of the lower desires and the development of the spiritual nature. Now, the idea which is the basis of all desires and passions in a man is the conviction of his indissoluble association with a male body. If he can inoculate himself thoroughly with the idea that he is a woman, he can get rid of the ideas peculiar to his male body. Again, with the idea that he is a woman, he may in turn be made to give way to another higher idea, namely, that he is neither man nor woman, but the Impersonal Spirit. The Impersonal Spirit alone can enjoy real communion with the Impersonal God. Hence the highest realization of the Vaishnava draws close to the transcendental experience of the Vedantist."

away, the glass becomes the same as it was before. One cannot assimilate spiritual instruction unless one has already developed love of God."

VIJAY: "Is bhakti alone sufficient for the attainment of God, for His vision?"

MASTER: "Yes, one can see God through bhakti alone. But it must be 'ripe' bhakti, prema-bhakti and raga-bhakti. When one has that bhakti, one loves God even as the mother loves the child, the child the mother, or the wife the husband.[8]

"When one has such love for God, one doesn't feel any physical attraction to wife, children, relatives, and friends. One retains only compassion for them. To such a man the world appears often as a foreign land, a place where he has merely to perform his duties. It is like a man's having his real home in the country, but coming to Calcutta for work; he has to rent a house in Calcutta for the sake of his duties. When one develops love of God, one completely gets rid of one's attachment to the world and worldly wisdom.

"A man cannot see God if he has even the slightest trace of worldliness. Matchsticks, if damp, won't strike fire though you rub a thousand of them against the matchbox. You only waste a heap of sticks. The mind soaked in worldliness is like a damp matchstick.

"If the devotee but once feels this attachment, this ecstatic love for God, this mature devotion and longing, then he sees God in both His aspects: with form and without form."

VIJAY: "How can one see God?"

MASTER: "One cannot see God without purity of heart. Through attachment to 'woman' and 'gold' the mind becomes stained—covered with dirt, as it were. A magnet cannot attract a needle if the needle is covered with mud. Wash away the mud and the magnet will draw it. Likewise, the dirt of the mind can be washed away with the tears of our eyes. This stain is removed if one sheds tears of repentance and

9 This type of lantern had dark glass on three sides.

says, 'O God, I shall never again do a wicked thing.' Thereupon God, who is like the magnet, draws to Himself the mind, which is like the needle. Then the devotee goes into samadhi and obtains the vision of God.

"You may try thousands of times, but nothing can be achieved without God's grace. One cannot see God without His grace. Is it an easy thing to receive grace? One must altogether renounce egotism; one cannot see God as long as one feels, 'I am the doer.'

"God doesn't easily appear in the heart of a man who feels himself to be his own master. But God can be seen the moment His grace descends. He is the Sun of Knowledge. One single ray of His has illumined the world with the light of knowledge. That is how we are able to see one another and acquire varied knowledge. One can see God only if He turns His light toward His own face.

"The police sergeant goes his rounds in the dark of night with a lantern[9] in his hand. No one sees his face; but with the help of that light the sergeant sees everybody's face, and others, too, can see one another. If you want to see the sergeant, however, you must pray to him: 'Sir, please turn the light on your own face. Let me see you.' In the same way one must pray to God: 'O Lord, be gracious and turn the light of knowledge on Thyself, that I may see Thy face.' A house without light indicates poverty. So one must light the lamp of Knowledge in one's heart."

[226–34]

1 | A *goswami* is a Vaishnava priest.

2 | *Mussalmans* is the term for "Muslims" in the Hindi and Urdu languages.

12 □ Realizing God

GOSWAMI:[1] "Sir, the chanting of God's name is enough. The scriptures emphasize the sanctity of God's name for the Kali Yuga."

MASTER: "Yes, there is no doubt about the sanctity of God's name. But can a mere name achieve anything, without the yearning of the devotee behind it? One should feel great restlessness of soul for the vision of God. Suppose a man repeats God's name mechanically, while his mind is absorbed in 'woman' and 'gold.' Can he achieve anything?

"Suppose a man becomes pure by chanting God's holy name, but immediately afterwards commits many sins. He has no strength of mind. He doesn't take a vow not to repeat his sins. A bath in the Ganges undoubtedly absolves one of all sins; but what does that avail? They say that the sins perch on the trees along the bank of the Ganges. No sooner does the man come back from the holy waters than the old sins jump on his shoulders from the trees. (All laugh.) The same old sins take possession of him again. He is hardly out of the water before they fall upon him.

"Therefore I say, chant God's name, and with it pray to Him that you may have love for Him. Pray to God that your attachment to such transitory things as wealth, name, and creature comforts may become less and less every day.

(To the goswami) "With sincerity and earnestness one can realize God through all religions. The Vaishnavas will realize God, and so will the Shaktas, the Vedantists, and the Brahmos. The Mussalmans[2] and Christians will realize Him too. All will certainly realize God if they are earnest and sincere.

⊙ "It has been recognized in the most ancient times that there are various forms of worshiping God. It is also recognized that different natures require different methods. Your method of coming to God may not be my method, possibly it might hurt me. Such an idea as that there is but one way for everybody is injurious, meaningless, and entirely to be avoided. Woe unto the world when everyone is of the same religious opinion and takes to the same path. Then all religions and all thought will be destroyed. Variety is the very soul of life. When it dies out entirely, creation will die. When this variation in thought is kept up, we must exist; and we need not quarrel because of that variety. Your way is very good for you but not for me. My way is good for me but not for you."

—Swami Vivekananda

"Some people indulge in quarrels, saying, 'One cannot attain anything unless one worships our Krishna,' or, 'Nothing can be gained without the worship of Kali, our Divine Mother,' or, 'One cannot be saved without accepting the Christian religion.' This is pure dogmatism. The dogmatist says, 'My religion alone is true, and the religions of others are false.' This is a bad attitude. God can be reached by many different paths.

"Further, some say that God has form and is not formless. Thus they start quarreling. A Vaishnava quarrels with a Vedantist.

"One can rightly speak of God only after one has seen Him. He who has seen God knows really and truly that God has form and that He is formless as well. He has many other aspects that cannot be described.

"Once some blind men chanced to come near an animal that someone told them was an elephant. They were asked what the elephant was like. The blind men began to feel its body. One of them said the elephant was like a pillar; he had touched only its leg. Another said it was like a winnowing fan; he had touched only its ear. In this way the others, having touched its tail or belly, gave their different versions of the elephant. Just so, a man who has seen only one aspect of God limits God to that alone. It is his conviction that God cannot be anything else.

(To the goswami) "How can you say that the only truth about God is that He has form? It is undoubtedly true that God comes down to earth in a human form, as in the case of Krishna. And it is true as well that God reveals Himself to His devotees in various forms. But it is also true that God is formless; He is the Indivisible Existence-Knowledge-Bliss Absolute. He has been described in the Vedas both as formless and as endowed with form. He is also described there both as attributeless and as endowed with attributes."

[239–41]

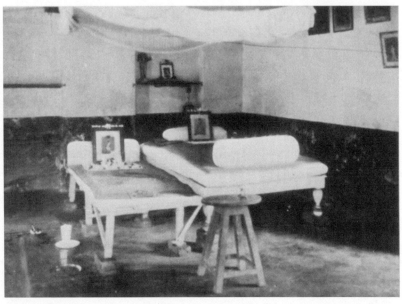

Sri Ramakrishna's room. He talked to the devotees from the smaller couch and slept on the larger couch.

13 □ Beyond Good and Evil

It was Sunday morning. The Master, looking like a boy, was seated in his room, and near him was another boy, his beloved disciple Rakhal. M entered and saluted the Master. Ramlal also was in the room, and Kishori, Manilal Mallick, and several other devotees gathered by and by.

Mallick, a businessman, had recently been to Benares, where he owned a bungalow.

MASTER: "So you have been to Benares. Did you see any holy men there?"

MANILAL: "Yes, sir. I paid my respects to Trailanga Swami, Bhaskarananda, and others. Trailanga Swami keeps a strict vow of silence. Unlike him, Bhaskarananda is friendly with all."

MASTER: "Did you have any conversation with Bhaskarananda?"

MANILAL: "Yes, sir. We had a long talk. Among other things we discussed the problem of good and evil. He said to me: 'Don't follow the path of evil. Give up sinful thoughts. That is how God wants us to act. Perform only those duties that are virtuous.'"

MASTER: "Yes, that is also a path, meant for the worldly-minded. But those whose spiritual consciousness has been awakened, who have realized that God alone is real and all else is illusory, cherish a different ideal. They are aware that God alone is the Doer and others are His instruments.

"Those whose spiritual consciousness has been awakened never make a false step. They do not have to reason in order to shun evil. They are so full of love of God that whatever action they undertake

1   "Beyond virtue and vice": see n. 4, p. 30.

is a good action. They are fully conscious that they are not the doers of their actions, but mere servants of God.

"Fully awakened souls are beyond virtue and vice.[1] They realize that it is God who does everything.

"There was a monastery in a certain place. The monks residing there went out daily to beg their food. One day a monk, while out for his alms, saw a landlord beating a man mercilessly. The compassionate monk stepped in and asked the landlord to stop. But the landlord was filled with anger and turned his wrath against the innocent monk. He beat the monk till he fell unconscious on the ground. Someone reported the matter to the monastery. The monks ran to the spot and found their brother lying there. Four or five of them carried him back and laid him on a bed. He was still unconscious. The other monks sat around him sad at heart; some were fanning him. Finally someone suggested that he should be given a little milk to drink. When it was poured into his mouth he regained consciousness. He opened his eyes and looked around. One of the monks said, 'Let us see whether he is fully conscious and can recognize us.' Shouting into his ear, he said, 'Revered sir, who is giving you milk?' 'Brother,' replied the holy man in a low voice, 'He who beat me is now giving me milk.'

"But one does not attain such a state of mind without the realization of God."

[243–46]

@ "If you seek God, then seek Him in man; He manifests Himself more in man than in any other thing. If you see a man endowed with ecstatic love, overflowing with prema, mad after God, intoxicated with His love, then know for certain that God has incarnated Himself through that man."

—Sri Ramakrishna *[371]*

14 □ A Yearning Heart

The worship was over in the temples and the bells rang for the food offerings in the shrines. As it was a summer noon, the sun was very hot. The flood tide started in the Ganges and a breeze came up from the south. Sri Ramakrishna was resting in his room after his meal.

Presently a few elderly members of the Brahmo Samaj arrived. The room was full of devotees. Sri Ramakrishna was sitting on his bed, facing the north. He kept smiling, and talked to the Brahmo devotees in a joyous mood.

MASTER: "You talk glibly about prema. But is it such a commonplace thing? There are two characteristics of prema, ecstatic love of God. First, it makes a man forget the world. So intense is his love of God that he becomes unconscious of outer things. Second, he has no feeling of 'my-ness' toward the body, which is dear to all. He wholly gets rid of the feeling that the body is the soul.

"There are certain signs of God-realization. A man who longs for God is not far from attaining Him. What are the outer indications of such longing? They are discrimination, dispassion, compassion for living beings, serving holy men, loving their company, chanting God's name and glories, telling the truth, and the like. When you see those signs in an aspirant, you can rightly say that for him the vision of God is not far to seek.

"The state of a servant's house will tell you unmistakably if his master has decided to visit it. First, the rubbish and jungle around the house are cleared up. Second, the soot and dirt are removed from the rooms. Third, the courtyard, floors, and other places are swept

1 *Vichara,* a practice of *jnana yoga,* entails reflection or inquiry within. An example of it is the formulation *neti, neti* (see n. 14, p. 40).

2 The inner organs are mind *(manas);* intelligence *(buddhi);* "mind-stuff," the repository of impressions created by our actions *(chitta);* and ego or sense of "I" *(ahamkara).*

clean. Finally the master himself sends various things to the house, such as a carpet, a hubble-bubble for smoking, and the like. When you see these things coming, you conclude that the master will very soon arrive."

A DEVOTEE: "Sir, should one first practice discrimination to attain self-control?"

MASTER: "That is also a path. It is called the path of vichara, reasoning.[1] But the inner organs[2] are brought under control through the path of devotion as well. This self-control is rather easily accomplished that way. Sense pleasures appear more and more tasteless as love for God grows."

DEVOTEE: "How can I develop love for God?"

MASTER: "Repeat His name, and sins will disappear. Thus you will destroy lust, anger, the desire for creature comforts, and so on."

DEVOTEE: "How can I take delight in God's name?"

MASTER: "Pray to God with a yearning heart that you may take delight in His name. He will certainly fulfill your heart's desire.

"As is a man's feeling, so is his gain. Once two friends were going along the street when they saw some people listening to a reading of the *Bhagavata*. 'Come, friend,' said the one to the other. 'Let us hear the sacred book.' So saying he went in and sat down. The second man peeped in and went away. He entered a house of ill fame. But very soon he felt disgusted with the place. 'Shame on me!' he said to himself. 'My friend has been listening to the sacred words about Hari; and see where I am!' But the friend who had been listening to the *Bhagavata* also became disgusted. 'What a fool I am!' he said. 'I have been listening to this fellow's blah-blah, and my friend is having a grand time.' In the course of time they both died. The messenger of Death came for the soul of the one who had listened to the *Bhagavata*

One of the many contemporary representations of Kali, the Divine Mother

and dragged it off to hell. The messenger of God came for the soul of the other, who had been to the house of prostitution, and led it up to heaven.

"Verily, the Lord looks into a man's heart and does not judge him by what he does or where he lives."

[245–46]

1 Once one has "seen through" the attachment to pleasure, renunciation occurs naturally.

15 □ What Is the Way?

Sri Ramakrishna paid a visit to Benimadhav Pal's garden house at Sinthi, near Calcutta, on the occasion of the semiannual festival of the Brahmo Samaj. Many devotees of the Samaj were present and sat around the Master. Now and then some of them asked him questions.

A BRAHMO DEVOTEE: "Sir, what is the way?"

MASTER: "Attachment to God, or, in other words, love for Him. And secondly, prayer."

BRAHMO DEVOTEE: "Which one is the way—love or prayer?"

MASTER: "First love and then prayer."

Continuing, the Master said: "And one must always chant God's name and glories and pray to Him. An old metal pot must be scrubbed every day. What is the use of cleaning it only once? Further, one must practice discrimination and renunciation; one must be conscious of the unreality of the world."

BRAHMO: "Is it good to renounce the world?"

MASTER: "Not for all. Those who have not yet come to the end of their enjoyments should not renounce the world."

BRAHMO: "What is the meaning of the 'end of enjoyments'?"

MASTER: "I mean the enjoyment of 'woman' and 'gold.' Most people don't feel any longing for God unless they have once passed through the experience of wealth, name, fame, creature comforts, and the like, that is to say, unless they have seen through these enjoyments."[1]

@ "He who has realized God does not look upon a woman with the eye of lust; so he is not afraid of her. He perceives clearly that women are but so many aspects of the Divine Mother. He worships them all as the Mother Herself."

—Sri Ramakrishna *[225]*

2 Mahamaya, the inscrutable power of Illusion (Maya), contains all the opposites of experience, such as knowledge and ignorance, good and evil. There can never be only knowledge or only ignorance in the relative world, because the play of duality is the Mother's Will. Since absolute Reality is nondual, both knowledge and ignorance are ultimately illusory. But while the "illusion of ignorance" leads to bondage, the "illusion of knowledge" leads to liberation.

3 The five elements are related to the five senses: earth/smell, water/taste, air/touch, fire/sight, and ether (space)/hearing. See also n. 6, p. 60.

BRAHMO: "Who is really bad, man or woman?"

MASTER: "As there are women endowed with spiritual knowledge, so also there are women who are ignorant. A woman endowed with knowledge leads a man to God, but a woman who is the embodiment of delusion makes him forget God and drowns him in the ocean of worldliness.

"This universe is created by the Mahamaya of God. Mahamaya contains both vidya-maya, the illusion of knowledge, and avidya-maya, the illusion of ignorance.[2] Through the help of vidya-maya one cultivates such virtues as the taste for holy company, knowledge, devotion, love, and renunciation. Avidya-maya consists of the five elements[3] and the objects of the five senses—form, flavor, smell, touch, and sound. These make one forget God."

BRAHMO: "If the power of avidya is the cause of ignorance, then why has God created it?"

MASTER: "That is His play. The glory of light cannot be appreciated without darkness. Happiness cannot be understood without misery. Knowledge of good is possible because of knowledge of evil.

"Further, the mango grows and ripens on account of the covering skin. You throw away the skin when the mango is fully ripe and ready to be eaten. It is possible for a man to attain gradually to the Knowledge of Brahman because of the covering skin of maya. Maya in its aspects of vidya and avidya may be likened to the skin of the mango. Both are necessary."

BRAHMO: "How does one cultivate the spirit of dispassion? Why don't all attain it?"

MASTER: "Dispassion is not possible unless there is satiety through enjoyment. You can easily cajole a small child with candies or toys. But after eating the candies and finishing its play, it cries, 'I want to go to my mother.' Unless you take the child to its mother, it will throw away the toy and scream at the top of its voice."

4 According to the traditional guru system, the quest for spiritual knowledge is undertaken under the guidance of a qualified teacher, or guru, who initiates the disciple into spiritual practices.

5 The true guru is the Self within. The external teacher is simply a projection of It.

6 The Upanishads are ancient mystical writings, part of the scriptures known as the Vedas, which convey the "hidden meaning" of the Vedas concerning the spiritual goal of life and how to attain it. They are the basis of the teachings of Vedanta.

7 The serene attitude was characteristic of the *rishis* (seers) of ancient times, who had no desire for worldly enjoyment. On the other attitudes, see n. 8, p. 118.

The members of the Brahmo Samaj are opposed to the traditional guru system of orthodox Hinduism.[4] Therefore the Brahmo devotee asked the Master about it.

BRAHMO: "Is spiritual knowledge impossible without a guru?"

MASTER: "Satchidananda alone is the Guru.[5] If a man in the form of a guru awakens spiritual consciousness in you, then know for certain that it is God the Absolute who has assumed that human form for your sake. The guru is like a companion who leads you by the hand. After realizing God, one loses the distinction between the guru and the disciple. The relationship between them remains as long as the disciple does not see God."

After dusk the preacher of the Brahmo Samaj conducted the service from the pulpit. The service was interspersed with recitations from the Upanishads[6] and the singing of Brahmo songs.

After the service the Master and the preacher conversed.

MASTER: "It seems to me that both the formless Deity and God with form are real. What do you say?"

PREACHER: "Sir, I compare the formless God to the electric current, which is not seen with the eyes but can be felt."

MASTER: "Yes, both are true. God with form is as real as God without form. Do you know what the describing of God as formless only is like? It is like a man's playing only a monotone on his flute, though it has seven holes. But on the same instrument another man plays different melodies. Likewise, in how many ways the believers in a Personal God enjoy Him! They enjoy Him through many different attitudes: the serene attitude,[7] the attitude of a servant, a friend, a mother, a husband, or a lover.

"The nature of Brahman cannot be described. About It one remains silent. Who can explain the Infinite in words? However high a bird may soar, there are regions higher still.

"Once four friends, in the course of a walk, saw a place enclosed by a wall. The wall was very high. They all became eager to know what was inside. One of them climbed to the top of the wall. What he saw on looking inside made him speechless with wonder. He only cried, 'Ah! Ah!' and jumped in. He could not give any information about what he saw. The others, too, climbed the wall, uttered the same cry, 'Ah! Ah!,' and jumped in. Now who could tell what was inside?"

—Sri Ramakrishna *[266]*

"After having the vision of God, man is overpowered with bliss. He becomes silent. Who will speak? Who will explain?"

PREACHER: "Yes, sir, it is so described in Vedanta."

MASTER: "Under the spell of God's maya man forgets his true nature. He forgets that he is heir to the infinite glories of his Father. This divine maya is made up of three gunas. And all three are robbers; for they rob man of all his treasures and make him forget his true nature. The three gunas are sattva, rajas, and tamas. Of these, sattva alone points the way to God. But even sattva cannot take a man to God.

"Let me tell you a story. Once a rich man was passing through a forest, when three robbers surrounded him and robbed him of everything he had. Then one of the robbers said: 'What's the good of keeping the man alive? Kill him.' He was about to strike their victim with his sword, when the second robber intervened and said: 'There's no use in killing him. Let us bind him fast and leave him here. Then he won't be able to tell the police.' Accordingly the robbers tied him with a rope and went away.

"After a while the third robber returned to the rich man and said: 'Ah! You're badly hurt, aren't you? Come, I'm going to release you.' The robber set the man free and led him out of the forest. When they came near the highway, the robber said, 'Follow this road and you will reach home easily.' 'But you must come with me too,' said the man. 'You have done so much for me. All my people will be happy to see you.' 'No,' said the robber, 'it is not possible for me to go there. The police will arrest me.' So saying, he left the rich man after pointing out his way.

"Now, the first robber, who said: 'What's the good of keeping the man alive? Kill him,' is tamas. It destroys. The second robber is rajas, which binds a man to the world and entangles him in a variety of activities. Rajas makes him forget God. Sattva alone shows the way to God. It produces virtues like compassion, righteousness, and

@ "Through unselfish action one finally acquires pure sattva. Sattva mixed with rajas diverts the mind to various objects. From it springs the conceit of doing good to the world. To do good to the world is extremely difficult for such an insignificant creature as man. But there is no harm in doing good to others in an unselfish spirit. This is called unselfish action. It is highly beneficial for a person to try to perform such action. But by no means all succeed, for it is very difficult. Everyone must work. Only one or two can renounce action. Rarely do you find a man who has developed pure sattva. Through disinterested action sattva mixed with rajas gradually turns into pure sattva."

—Sri Ramakrishna

devotion. Again, sattva is like the last step of the stairs. Next to it is the roof. The Supreme Brahman is man's own abode. One cannot attain the Knowledge of Brahman unless one transcends the three gunas."

PREACHER: "You have given us a fine talk, sir."

MASTER (*with a smile*): "You are a preacher and teach so many people! You are a steamship and I am a mere fishing boat." (*All laugh.*)

[251–56]

1 A pundit (Hindi, *pandit*) is a Sanskrit scholar. Ramakrishna had an aversion to those scholars who were proud of their learning yet who were engrossed in worldly desires. Pundi Shashadhar, however, was a sincere seeker of God.

2 A *seer* is approximately a kilogram. *Sandesh* are sweetmeats. The wearing-cloth is used for a simple wrapped and pleated men's garment called a *dhoti.*

16 □ Reading, Hearing, and Seeing

Sri Ramakrishna was in his room, sitting on a mat spread on the floor. Pundit Shashadhar and a few devotees were with him on the mat, and the rest sat on the bare floor. . . . The pundit[1] had studied the Vedas and other scriptures. He loved to discuss philosophy. The Master. . . cast his benign look on the pundit and gave him counsel through parables.

MASTER (to the pundit): "There are many scriptures like the Vedas. But one cannot realize God without austerity and spiritual discipline. 'God cannot be found in the six systems, the Vedas, or the Tantra.'

"But one should learn the contents of the scriptures and then act according to their injunctions. Once a man lost a letter. He couldn't remember where he had left it. He began to search for it with a lamp. After two or three people had searched, the letter was at last found. The message in the letter was: 'Please send us five seers of sandesh and a piece of wearing-cloth.'[2] The man read it and then threw the letter away. There was no further need of it; now all he had to do was to buy the five seers of sandesh and the piece of cloth.

"Better than reading is hearing, and better than hearing is seeing. One understands the scriptures better by hearing them from the lips of the guru or of a holy man. Then one doesn't have to think about their nonessential part.

"But seeing is far better than hearing. Then all doubts disappear. It is true that many things are recorded in the scriptures; but all these are useless without the direct realization of God, without devotion to His Lotus Feet, without purity of heart. The almanac forecasts the rainfall of the year. But not a drop of water will you get by squeezing the almanac. No, not even one drop."

3 The momentum that keeps the present body alive was created by the actions of the person's previous birth.

4 *Jada-samadhi* is defined as "communion with God in which the aspirant appears lifeless, like an inert object."

A DEVOTEE: "Does the body remain even after the realization of God?"

MASTER: "The present body remains alive as long as its momentum[3] is not exhausted; but future births are no longer possible. The wheel moves as long as the impulse that has set it in motion lasts. Then it comes to a stop. In the case of such a person, passions like lust and anger are burnt up. Only the body remains alive to perform a few actions."

The Master remained silent a few moments and then asked Pundit Shashadhar to have a smoke. The pundit went to the southeast veran-dah to smoke. Soon he came back to the room and sat on the floor with the devotees. Seated on the small couch, the Master continued the conversation.

MASTER (to the pundit): "Let me tell you something. There are three kinds of ananda, joy: the joy of worldly enjoyment, the joy of worship, and the Joy of Brahman. The joy of worldly enjoyment is the joy of 'woman' and 'gold,' which people always love. The joy of worship one feels while chanting God's name and glories. And the Joy of Brahman is the joy of God-vision. After experiencing the joy of God-vision, the rishis of olden times went beyond all rules and conventions.

"What is samadhi? It is the complete merging of the mind in God-Consciousness. The jnani experiences jada-samadhi,[4] in which no trace of 'I' is left. The samadhi attained through the path of bhakti is called chetana-samadhi. In this samadhi there remains the Consciousness of 'I'—the 'I' of the servant-and-Master relationship, of the lover-and-Beloved relationship, of the enjoyer-and-Food rela-tionship. God is the Master; the devotee is the servant. God is the Beloved; the devotee is the lover. God is the Food; and the devotee is the enjoyer. 'I don't want to be sugar. I want to eat it.'

"God keeps a little of 'I' in his devotee even after giving him the Knowledge of Brahman. That 'I' is the 'I' of the devotee, the 'I' of the jnani. Through that 'I' the devotee enjoys the infinite play of God.

5 *Lila* (pronounced *leela*) is the play of creation. To awakened consciousness, the entire universe, with all its joys and sorrows, pleasures and pains, appears as a divine game, sport, or drama. It is a play in which the one Consciousness performs all the roles. Alluding to this *lila* of the Divine Mother, Ramakrishna called the physical universe a "mansion of mirth."

6 Sri Ramakrishna loved the dream of Maya dismissed by the orthodox Vedantists. In a vision, Kali had told him not to lose himself in the featureless Absolute but to remain in *bhava-mukha,* the threshold of relative consciousness.

"It is a joy to merge the mind in the Indivisible Brahman through contemplation. And it is also a joy to keep the mind on the Lila,[5] the Relative, without dissolving it in the Absolute.

"A mere jnani is a monotonous person. He always analyzes, saying: 'It is not this, not this. The world is like a dream.'"[6]

[309, 310–12]

1 Ramakrishna acted with childlike curiosity in response to simple desires that arose in his mind, as described in this passage—for sweets, ornaments, smoking, and so on. For the spiritual aspirant, however, the desire for worldly enjoyments is considered a major obstacle to liberation according to the more ascetic Hindu traditions, which teach control and detachment. As Swami Vivekananda has written, "A perfect, free being cannot have any desire. God cannot want anything. If He desired, He could not be God; He would be imperfect. . . . Therefore it has been taught by all teachers: 'Desire nothing. Give up all desires and be perfectly satisfied.'"

Sri Ramakrishna's teaching emphasizes the transmutation of all wants into one—the restless longing for God, which leads to an effortless letting go of all other desires. But this natural process does not begin to unfold until one has exhausted the momentum of habitual cravings—or unless one receives the grace of a Master. Several of Ramakrishna's close followers appear to have had their desires transformed in this way through their contact with him.

2 Sri Ramakrishna was unable to touch money without writhing in pain. He said, "My hand gets all twisted up if I hold money in it; my breathing stops. But there is no harm in spending money to lead a spiritual life in the world—if one spends it, for instance, in the worship of God and the service of holy men and devotees."

17 □ Desire

MAHENDRA: "Why does one slip from the path of yoga?"

MASTER: "While thinking of God the aspirant may feel a craving for material enjoyment. It is this craving that makes him slip from the path. In his next life he will be born with the spiritual tendencies that he failed to translate into action in his present life."

MAHENDRA: "Then what is the way?"

MASTER: "No salvation is possible for a man as long as he has desire, as long as he hankers for worldly things.

"It is not good to cherish desires and hankerings. For that reason I used to fulfill whatever desires came to my mind.[1] Once I saw some colored sweetmeats at Burrabazar and wanted to eat them. They brought me the sweets and I ate a great many. The result was that I fell ill.

"In my boyhood days, while bathing in the Ganges, I saw a boy with a gold ornament around his waist. During my state of divine intoxication I felt a desire to have a similar ornament myself. I was given one, but I couldn't keep it on very long. When I put it on, I felt within my body the painful uprush of a current of air. It was because I had touched gold to my skin.[2] I wore the ornament a few moments and then had to put it aside. Otherwise I should have had to tear it off.

"At that time many holy men used to visit the temple garden. A desire arose in my mind that there should be a separate storeroom to supply them with their provisions. Mathur Babu arranged for one.

3 *Rajas* is one of the three gunas, or subtle energies of nature (see n. 19, p. 42). It is the force of passion and action that motivates us to seek happiness in external pursuit of pleasure, wealth, and power. It creates conflict, suffering, and agitation.

The sadhus were given foodstuffs, fuel, and the like from that store-room.

"Once the idea came to me to put on a very expensive robe embroidered with gold and to smoke a silver hubble-bubble. Mathur Babu sent me the new robe and the hubble-bubble. I put on the robe. I also smoked the hubble-bubble in various fashions. Sometimes I smoked reclining this way, and sometimes that way, sometimes with head up, and sometimes with head down. Then I said to myself, 'O mind, this is what they call smoking a silver hubble-bubble.' Immediately I renounced it. I kept the robe on my body a few minutes longer and then took it off. I began to trample it underfoot and spit on it, saying: 'So this is an expensive robe! But it only increases a man's rajas.'"3

[325–26]

1 Sri Ramakrishna here associates the different phases of his spiritual practice *(sadhana)* with sacred texts of the various Hindu traditions: his devotional practices with the Puranas, scriptures of the Vaishnavas; his Tantric practices with the Tantras of the Shaktas (see n. 2 below); and his Vedantic practices with the Vedas. He also refers to the places where he performed his meditations: the Panchavati, his grove of five sacred trees; the *tulsi,* or sacred basil, a plant sacred to Vishnu; and the *bel* tree, sacred to Lord Shiva.

2 *Tantra* refers to both the texts and teachings of Tantrism. One translation of this Sanskrit word is "continuum," which reflects a basic principle of Tantra: there is a seamless continuity between spirit and matter, and Divinity manifests in all the pairs of opposites, both the "bad" and the "good." The aim of Tantra, in the words of Isherwood, is "to see, behind all phenomena, the presence of God," and the Tantric disciplines are "designed to help the aspirant overcome some particular form of attraction or aversion and realize the indwelling Godhead." Among the various practices of Tantra are sexual rituals requiring a partner of the opposite sex. Sri Ramakrishna, however, "proved that even the severest of [Tantric] disciplines could be practiced in complete chastity."

3 For a high-caste brahmin such as Ramakrishna to share food with a dog would be considered outrageously improper in the orthodox Hindu tradition, but such violation of social customs is characteristic of Tantrism. In his divinely intoxicated state, Ramakrishna saw everything as God.

18 □ Practicing the Disciplines

MASTER: ..."God made me pass through the disciplines of various paths.[1] First according to the Purana, then according to the Tantra.[2] I also followed the disciplines of the Vedas. At first I practiced sadhana in the Panchavati. I made a grove of tulsi plants and used to sit inside it and meditate. Sometimes I cried with a longing heart, 'Mother! Mother!' Or again, 'Rama! Rama!'

"I practiced the discipline of the Tantra under the bel tree. At that time I could see no distinction between the sacred tulsi and any other plant. Sometimes I rode on a dog and fed him with luchi, also eating part of the bread myself.[3] I realized that the whole world was filled with God alone.

(continued on page 159)

4 A *sannyasi* (or *sannyasin*), as a renouncer, has taken a vow of home-lessness and thus would not take his meals inside a house.

From the time he first started to worship Kali as a temple priest, Sri Ramakrishna began to have a variety of visions and other unusual spiritual experiences. His divine moods would cause him sometimes to be motionless, withdrawn into an internal state; on other occasions to appear like a happy and peaceful child; at still other times to enjoy deep ecstasy or behave like a madman—but it was the madness of divine love, not psychosis. Sometimes he would lose normal consciousness and perceive everything dissolved into a blissful, dazzling ocean of light. As he practiced various spiritual disciplines, he had visions of Hindu deities and incarnations—such as Kali, Krishna, Radha, Rama, Sita, Hanuman, and Chaitanya—and also of Muhammad, Jesus, and the Buddha. Often he would behold the presence of the Divine Mother in a woman—no matter whether she was a young village girl, his wife, or a prostitute.

In most cases it is not possible to interpret definitively the unique and mysterious visions of a great spiritual personality such as Rama-krishna; we simply read them with a sense of wonder. As a general comment, it might be said that some visions, such as those involving lights or divine forms, are associated with the planes of consciousness (see Ramakrishna's comments on pp. 97 and 99). In Vedanta it is taught that no visions occur at the highest state of God-realization, and seekers are advised not to talk about or give great importance to spiritual experiences that they may encounter on the way to the supreme goal. Ramakrishna, however, may have described his experiences for special reasons of his own, in order to guide and help his devotees and disciples.

"While practicing the disciplines of the Vedas I became a sannyasi. I used to lie down in the chandni and say to Hriday: 'I am a sannyasi. I shall take my meals here.'**4**

"I vowed to the Divine Mother that I would kill myself if I did not see God. I said to Her: 'O Mother, I am a fool. Please teach me what is contained in the Vedas, the Puranas, the Tantras, and the other scriptures.' The Mother said to me, 'The essence of the Vedanta is that Brahman alone is real and the world illusory.' The essence of the *Gita* is what you get by repeating the word ten times. It is reversed into *tagi*, which refers to renunciation.

"After the realization of God, how far below lie the Vedas, Vedanta, the Puranas, and Tantra! *(To Hazra)* I cannot utter the word 'Om' in samadhi. Why is that? I cannot say 'Om' unless I come down very far from the state of samadhi.

"I had all the experiences that one should have, according to the scriptures, after one's direct perception of God. I behaved like a child, like a madman, like a ghoul, and like an inert thing.

"I saw the visions described in the scriptures. Sometimes I saw the universe filled with sparks of fire. Sometimes I saw all the quarters glittering with light, as if the world were a lake of mercury. Sometimes I saw the world as if made of liquid silver. Sometimes, again, I saw all the quarters illumined as if with the light of Roman candles. So you see my experiences tally with those described in the scriptures.

(continued on page 161)

5   Evolution is the cosmic process by which the one indivisible Reality manifests all the forms of the phenomenal world. Involution is the reverse process, in which all forms return to the unmanifest state at the time of the dissolution of the universe. It may also refer to the process that begins when the individualized soul begins the spiritual journey, traversing the seven planes of consciousness, and culminates in the conscious experience of oneness with Brahman.

"It was revealed to me further that God Himself has become the universe and all its living beings and the twenty-four cosmic principles. It is like the process of evolution and involution.[5]

"Oh, what a state God kept me in at that time! One experience would hardly be over before another overcame me.

"I would see God in meditation, in the state of samadhi, and I would see the same God when my mind came back to the outer world. When looking at this side of the mirror I would see Him alone, and when looking on the reverse side I saw the same God."

[332–34]

1 Balaram Bose was a devotee from a wealthy Vaishnava family of Calcutta.

2 Girish Ghosh, one of the Master's householder devotees, was a celebrated dramatist of his day. A notorious drunkard and patron of brothels who was nonetheless attracted into Ramakrishna's orbit, he was transformed into a true lover of God. Although Ramakrishna never demanded that Girish give up alcohol, Girish overcame the habit himself, under the Master's influence. Among Girish's innovations in the Bengali theater was his introduction of women actors to perform the female roles, which had traditionally been played by males.

19 □ Divine Incarnation

. . . M went to Balaram's[1] house and found the Master sitting in the drawing room, surrounded by his devotees and disciples. The Master's face was beaming with a sweet smile, which was reflected in the happy faces of those in the room. . . .

GIRISH:[2] "Narendra says that God is infinite; we cannot even so much as say that the things or persons we perceive are parts of God. How can Infinity have parts? It cannot."

MASTER: "However great and infinite God may be, His Essence can and does manifest itself through man by His mere will. God's Incarnation as a man cannot be explained by analogy. One must feel it for oneself and realize it by direct perception. An analogy can give us only a little glimpse. By touching the horns, legs, or tail of a cow, we in fact touch the cow herself; but for us the essential thing about a cow is her milk, which comes through the udder. The Divine Incarnation is like the udder. God incarnates Himself as man from time to time in order to teach people devotion and divine love."

GIRISH: "Narendra says: 'Is it ever possible to know all of God? He is infinite.'"

MASTER (to Girish): "Who can comprehend everything about God? It is not given to man to know any aspect of God, great or small. And what need is there to know everything about God? It is enough if we only see Him. And we see God Himself if we but see His Incarnation. Suppose a person goes to the Ganges and touches its water. He will then say, 'Yes, I have seen and touched the Ganges.'

3 │ The eight occult powers (*mahasiddhi*s) are identified differently by various scriptures of Tantra and Yoga. They include such marvels as the ability to make oneself very tiny or very huge, become invisible, and enter another's body; the power to cure diseases; mastery over wild animals; and performing miracles such as raising the dead. For a lover of God, the desire for miraculous powers is considered a serious obstacle to spiritual progress because powers lead to subtle feelings of self-importance.

To say this it is not necessary for him to touch the whole length of the river from Hardwar to Gangasagar. (*Laughter.*)

"If I touch your feet, surely that is the same as touching you. (*Laughter.*) If a person goes to the ocean and touches but a little of its water, he has surely touched the ocean itself. Fire, as an element, exists in all things, but in wood it is present to a greater degree.". . .

The devotees seated in the room looked at Sri Ramakrishna as he began to chant the sweet name of the Divine Mother. After the chanting he began to pray. What was the need of prayer to a soul in constant communion with God? Did he not rather want to teach erring mortals how to pray? Addressing the Divine Mother, he said: "O Mother, I throw myself on Thy mercy; I take shelter at Thy Hallowed Feet. I do not want bodily comforts; I do not crave name and fame; I do not seek the eight occult powers.[3] Be gracious and grant that I may have pure love for Thee, a love unsmitten by desire, untainted by any selfish ends—a love craved by the devotee for the sake of love alone. And grant me the favor, O Mother, that I may not be deluded by Thy world-bewitching maya, that I may never be attached to the world, to 'woman' and 'gold,' conjured up by Thy inscrutable maya! O Mother, there is no one but Thee whom I may call my own. Mother, I do not know how to worship; I am without austerity; I have neither devotion nor knowledge. Be gracious, Mother, and out of Thy infinite mercy grant me love for Thy Lotus Feet."

Every word of this prayer, uttered from the depths of his soul, stirred the minds of the devotees. The melody of his voice and the childlike simplicity of his face touched their hearts.

[*370–71, 373*]

1 Narayana is a name of the deity Vishnu, and Lakshmi is his consort. Vaikuntha is their celestial abode. As a divine couple, Lakshmi and Narayana are comparable to Radha and Krishna, signifying the perfect union between God and Shakti, the feminine personification of his creative power, without which He can do nothing.

20 □ To Receive God's Grace

MASTER: "It is on account of the ego that one is not able to see God. In front of the door of God's mansion lies the stump of ego. One cannot enter the mansion without jumping over the stump.

"There was once a man who had acquired the power to tame ghosts. One day, at his summons, a ghost appeared. The ghost said: 'Now tell me what you want me to do. The moment you cannot give me any work, I shall break your neck.' The man had many things to accomplish, and he had the ghost do them all, one by one. At last he could find nothing more for the ghost to do. 'Now,' said the ghost, 'I am going to break your neck.' 'Wait a minute,' said the man. 'I shall return presently.' He ran to his teacher and said: 'Revered sir, I am in great danger. This is my trouble.' And he told his teacher his trouble and asked, 'What shall I do now?' The teacher said: 'Do this. Tell the ghost to straighten this kinky hair.' The ghost devoted itself day and night to straightening the hair. But how could it make a kinky hair straight? The hair remained kinky.

"Likewise, the ego seems to vanish this moment, but it reappears the next. Unless one renounces the ego, one does not receive God's grace.

"A guardian is appointed only for a minor. A boy cannot safeguard his property; therefore the king assumes responsibility for him. God does not take over our responsibilities unless we renounce our ego.

"Once Lakshmi and Narayana[1] were seated in Vaikuntha, when Narayana suddenly stood up. Lakshmi had been stroking His feet. She said, 'Lord, where are You going?' Narayana answered: 'One of My devotees is in great danger. I must save him.' With these words

2 The devotee picking up the brick is like the ego asserting itself as the agent of action. We believe that we are the "doer," but in reality it is God alone who is all and does all. The story shows that when we surrender to that truth—when we "let go and let God"—then we are able to receive the grace and help of God, which is always available. When we let go of the false ego, not only can we receive divine help, but we can see and eventually realize our oneness with God.

3 Gauri was a great scholar who was one of the first to proclaim Sri Ramakrishna a divine incarnation. He said, "I am fully convinced that you are that Mine of Spiritual Power, only a small fraction of which descends on earth, from time to time, in the form of an Incarnation. . . . I feel it in my heart and I have the scriptures on my side. I am ready to prove it to anyone who challenges me." Sri Ramakrishna replied, "Well, it is you who say so; but, believe me, I know nothing about it."

4 Pratap Hazra was a devotee known for his argumentative and hyper-critical nature.

He went out. But He came back immediately. Lakshmi said, 'Lord, why have You returned so soon?' Narayana smiled and said: 'The devotee was going along the road overwhelmed with love for Me. Some washermen were drying clothes on the grass, and the devotee unknowingly walked over the clothes. At this the washermen chased him and were going to beat him with their sticks. So I ran out to protect him.' 'But why have You come back?' asked Lakshmi. Narayana laughed and said: 'I saw the devotee himself picking up a brick to throw at them. *(All laugh.)* So I came back.'"[2]

TRAILOKYA: "It is very difficult to get rid of the ego. People only think they are free from it."

MASTER: "Gauri[3] would not refer to himself as 'I' lest he should feel egotistic. He would say 'this' instead. I followed his example and would refer to myself as 'this' instead of 'I.' Instead of saying, 'I have eaten,' I would say, 'This has eaten.' Mathur noticed it and said one day: 'What is this, revered father? Why should you talk that way? Let them talk that way. They have their egotism. You are free from it; you don't have to talk like them.'

"During the stage of sadhana one should describe God by all His attributes. One day Hazra[4] said to Narendra: 'God is Infinity. Infinite is His splendor. Do you think He will accept your offerings of sweets and bananas or listen to your music? This is a mistaken notion of yours.' Narendra at once sank ten fathoms. So I said to Hazra, 'You villain! Where will these youngsters be if you talk to them like that?' How can a man live if he gives up devotion? No doubt God has infinite splendor; yet He is under the control of His devotees. A rich man's gatekeeper came to the parlor where his master was seated with his friends. He stood on one side of the room. In his hand he had something covered with a cloth. He was very hesitant. The master asked him, 'Well, gatekeeper, what have you in your hand?' Very hesitantly the servant took out a custard apple from under the cover,

Sri Ramakrishna said: "One day Keshab came here with his followers. They stayed till ten at night. We were all seated in the Panchavati. Pratap and several others said they would like to spend the night here. Keshab said: 'No, I must go. I have some work to do.' I laughed and said: 'Can't you sleep without the smell of your 'fish-basket'?' Once a fishwife was a guest in the house of a gardener who raised flowers. She came there with her empty basket, after selling fish in the market, and was asked to sleep in a room where flowers were kept. But because of the fragrance of the flowers she couldn't get to sleep for a long time. Her hostess saw her condition and said, 'Hello! Why are you tossing from side to side so restlessly?' The fishwife said: 'I don't know, friend. Perhaps the smell of the flowers has been disturbing my sleep. Can you give me my fish-basket? Perhaps that will put me to sleep.' The basket was brought to her. She sprinkled water on it and set it near her nose. Then she fell sound asleep and snored all night." *[301-2]*.

Swami Vivekananda says: "The world is our fish-basket. We must not depend upon it for enjoyment."

placed it in front of his master, and said, 'Sir, it is my desire that you eat this.' The master was impressed with his servant's devotion. With great love he took the fruit in his hand and said: 'Ah! This is a very nice custard apple. Where did you pick it? You must have taken a great deal of trouble to get it.'

"A man cannot renounce action as long as he desires worldly enjoyment. As long as one cherishes a desire for enjoyment, one performs action.

"A bird sat absent-mindedly on the mast of a ship anchored in the Ganges. Slowly the ship sailed out into the ocean. When the bird came to its senses, it could find no shore in any direction. It flew toward the north hoping to reach land; it went very far and grew very tired but could find no shore. What could it do? It returned to the ship and sat on the mast. After a long while the bird flew away again, this time toward the east. It couldn't find land in that direction either; everywhere it saw nothing but limitless ocean. Very tired, it again returned to the ship and sat on the mast. After resting a long while the bird went toward the south, and then toward the west. When it found no sign of land in any direction, it came back and settled down on the mast. It did not leave the mast again, but sat there without making any further effort. It no longer felt restless or worried. Because it was free from worry it made no further effort. . . .

"Worldly people wander about to the four quarters of the earth for the sake of happiness. They don't find it anywhere; they only become tired and weary. When through their attachment to 'woman' and 'gold' they only suffer misery, they feel an urge toward dispassion and renunciation. Most people cannot renounce 'woman' and 'gold' without first enjoying them.

"But what is there to enjoy in the world? The pleasure is only transitory. One moment it exists and the next moment it disappears.

"The world is like an overcast sky that steadily pours down rain: the face of the sun is seldom seen. There is mostly suffering in the

5 Sri Ramakrishna frequently refers to the feeling of urgent longing or passionate yearning as the key to the attainment of God-realization.

world. On account of the cloud of 'woman' and 'gold' one cannot see the sun. Some people ask me: 'Sir, why has God created such a world? Is there no way out for us?' I say to them: 'Why shouldn't there be a way out? Take shelter with God and pray to Him with a yearning heart for a favorable wind, that you may have things in your favor. If you call on Him with yearning,[5] He will surely listen to you."

[389–93]

1 *Mahakasha* (*maha*, great, plus *akasha*, ether), one of several types of "space," is the infinite luminous emptiness that contains everything.

2 Hrishikesh (or Rishikesh) is a village at the foot of the Himalayas, on the Ganges, where *sadhus* practice austerities.

3 The *sahasrara* represents the highest level of realization.

4 *Kundalini* is the power of inner consciousness, envisioned as a coiled-up serpent at the base of the spine. When this power is aroused (for example, through spiritual disciplines or by the touch of a perfect master), it rises up the spine through a subtle channel called the *sushumna*, passing through the seven main energy centers known as chakras, until it reaches the crown of the head. The chakras are spiritual rather than anatomical structures, representing ascending levels of consciousness. They are nonetheless correlated with parts of the body. The chakras include the *muladhara* (base of the spine, anus), *svadhisthana* (sexual organs), *manipura* (navel), *anahata* (heart), *visuddha* (throat), and *ajna* (the "third eye," between the eyebrows). The *sahasrara* (crown) is the summit of consciousness.

5 *Mahavayu* (*maha*, great, plus *vayu*, the principle of air or wind) refers to the subtle currents of vital energy *(prana)*.

21 □ Something Special

MASTER: "Well, some say that my soul, going into samadhi, flies about like a bird in the Mahakasha, the Infinite Space.[1]

"Once a sadhu of Hrishikesh[2] came here. He said to me: 'There are five kinds of samadhi. I find you have experienced them all. In these samadhis one feels the movement of the spiritual current to be like that of an ant, a fish, a monkey, a bird, or a serpent.'

"Sometimes the spiritual current rises through the spine, crawling like an ant.

"Sometimes, in samadhi, the soul swims joyfully in the ocean of divine ecstasy, like a fish.

"Sometimes, when I lie down on my side, I feel the spiritual current pushing me like a monkey and playing with me joyfully. I remain still. That current, like a monkey, suddenly with one jump reaches the Sahasrara.[3] That is why you see me jump up with a start.

"Sometimes, again, the spiritual current rises like a bird hopping from one branch to another. The place where it rests feels like fire. It hops from one center to another, and thus gradually to the head.

"Sometimes the spiritual current moves like a snake. Going up in a zigzag way, it at last reaches the head and I go into samadhi.

"A man's spiritual consciousness is not awakened unless his Kundalini[4] is aroused.

"The Kundalini dwells in the Muladhara. When it is aroused, it passes along the Sushumna nerve, goes through the centers of Svadhisthana, Manipura, and so on, and at last reaches the head. This is called the movement of the mahavayu,[5] the great spiritual current. It culminates in samadhi.

6 The centers are likened to lotuses in the scriptures, each with a different number of petals (related to its particular configuration of nerve channels, or *nadis*). In an unawakened person, the *kundalini* remains dormant and the "lotuses" droop down.

"One's spiritual consciousness is not awakened by the mere reading of books. One should also pray to God. The Kundalini is aroused if the aspirant feels restless for God. To talk of Knowledge from mere study and hearsay! What will that accomplish?

"Just before my attaining this state of mind it was revealed to me how the Kundalini is aroused, how the lotuses[6] of the different centers blossom forth, and how all this culminates in samadhi. This is a very secret experience. I saw a boy twenty-two or twenty-three years old, exactly resembling me, enter the Sushumna nerve and commune with the lotuses, touching them with his tongue. He began with the center at the anus and passed through the centers at the sexual organ, navel, and so on. The different lotuses of those centers—four-petaled, six-petaled, ten-petaled, and so forth—had been drooping. At his touch they stood erect.

"When he reached the heart—I distinctly remember it—and communed with the lotus there, touching it with his tongue, the twelve-petaled lotus, which was hanging head down, stood erect and opened its petals. Then he came to the sixteen-petaled lotus in the throat and the two-petaled lotus in the forehead. And last of all, the thousand-petaled lotus in the head blossomed. Since then I have been in this state."

Sri Ramakrishna came down to the floor and sat near Mahimacharan. M and a few other devotees were near him. Rakhal also was in the room.

MASTER (to Mahima): "For a long time I have wanted to tell you my spiritual experiences, but I could not. I feel like telling you today.

"You say that by mere sadhana one can attain a state of mind like mine. But it is not so. There is something special here [referring to himself]."

Rakhal, M, and the others became eager to hear what the Master was going to say.

7 The banyan, a member of the fig tree family, is one of the species in
the Panchavati, the grove of five sacred trees in the temple garden
where Ramakrishna had many of his visions. Its branches send out long
aerial roots that reach down to the earth and eventually become a massive new trunk. The banyan is said to be a favorite tree of Lord
Vishnu's. The bakul, not part of the Panchavati, was one of the other
trees in the garden.

8 Sri Ramakrishna referred to Indians who were influenced by Western ideas and education as "Englishmen."

MASTER: "God talked to me. It was not merely His vision. Yes, He talked to me. Under the banyan tree I saw Him coming from the Ganges. Then we laughed so much! By way of playing with me He cracked my fingers. Then He talked. Yes, He talked to me.

"For three days I wept continuously. And He revealed to me what is in the Vedas, the Puranas, the Tantras, and the other scriptures.

"One day He showed me the maya of Mahamaya. A small light inside a room began to grow, and at last it enveloped the whole universe.

"Further, He revealed to me a huge reservoir of water covered with green scum. The wind moved a little of the scum and immediately the water became visible; but in the twinkling of an eye, scum from all sides came dancing in and again covered the water. He revealed to me that the water was like Satchidananda, and the scum, like maya. On account of the maya, Satchidananda is not seen. Though now and then one may get a glimpse of It, again maya covers It.

"God reveals the nature of the devotees to me before they arrive. I saw Chaitanya's party singing and dancing near the Panchavati, between the banyan tree and the bakul tree.[7] I noticed Balaram there. If it weren't for him, who would there be to supply me with sugar candy and such things? *(Pointing to M)* And I saw him too.

"I had seen Keshab before I actually met him—I had seen him and his party in my samadhi. In front of me sat a roomful of men. Keshab looked like a peacock sitting with its tail spread out. The tail meant his followers. I saw a red gem on Keshab's head. That indicated his rajas. He said to his disciples, 'Please listen to what he [*meaning the Master*] is saying.' I said to the Divine Mother: 'Mother, these people hold the views of "Englishmen."'[8] Why should I talk to them?' Then the Mother explained to me that it would be like this in the Kali Yuga. Keshab and his followers got from here [*meaning himself*] the names of Hari and the Divine Mother."

(continued on page 181)

9 | In this vision, Ramakrishna beholds Brahman (referred to here as the Indivisible Satchidananda, "Existence-Knowledge-Bliss") in its two aspects, with and without form. His devotees who worship God with form are on one side of the fence, while Narendra is alone in the formless realm, enveloped in a reddish light (perhaps suggesting his fiery nature, just as the red gem in the preceding vision symbolizes *rajas,* the dynamic principle). Ramakrishna implies that he summoned Narendra out of his high meditative state, causing him to incarnate as a person of the *kayastha* caste (a Bengali subcaste), born in a section of Calcutta called Simla (Narendra's birthplace). The Master prays that his favorite disciple will remain in human form and not return to his original state of divine absorption, which is so transcendent that it frightens a devotee of the personal God.

10 | His illness was cancer. See n. 1, p. 186.

11 | Raghuvir is Lord Rama, the avatar of Vishnu, who was the family deity. Sri Ramakrishna's father had the prophetic dream in a temple dedicated to Vishnu at Gaya, a pilgrimage site in Bihar.

(*Pointing to himself*) "There must be something special here. . . . I have had many amazing visions. I had a vision of the Indivisible Satchidananda.[9] Inside It I saw two groups with a fence between them. On one side were Kedar, Chuni, and other devotees who believe in the Personal God. On the other side was a luminous space like a heap of red brick dust. Inside it was seated Narendra immersed in samadhi. Seeing him absorbed in meditation, I called aloud, 'Oh, Narendra!' He opened his eyes a little. I came to realize that he had been born, in another form, in Simla in a kayastha family. At once I said to the Divine Mother, 'Mother, entangle him in maya; otherwise he will give up his body in samadhi.' Kedar, a believer in the Personal God, peeped in and ran away with a shudder.

"Therefore I feel that it is the Divine Mother Herself who dwells in this body and plays with the devotees. When I first had my exalted state of mind, my body would radiate light. My chest was always flushed. Then I said to the Divine Mother: 'Mother, do not reveal Thyself outwardly. Please go inside.' That is why my complexion is so dull now. If my body were still luminous, people would have tormented me; a crowd would always have thronged here. Now there is no outer manifestation. That keeps weeds away. Only genuine devotees will remain with me now. Do you know why I have this illness?[10] It has the same significance. Those whose devotion to me has a selfish motive behind it will run away at the sight of my illness.

"I cherished a desire. I said to the Mother, 'O Mother, I shall be the king of the devotees.'

"Again, this thought arose in my mind: 'He who sincerely prays to God will certainly come here. He must.' You see, that is what is happening now. Only people of that kind come.

"My parents knew who dwells inside this body. Father had a dream at Gaya. In that dream Raghuvir said to him, 'I shall be born as your son.'[11]

(*continued on page 183*)

12 | *Nangta* means the "Naked One," the name Ramakrishna used for his guru Totapuri, a member of an ascetic Vedantic sect whose monks lived with only "space as clothing." Totapuri taught him the absolute non-dualism of Shankaracharya's Vedanta, which emphasizes the nameless, formless reality of Brahman, which alone exists. Ramakrishna said of him, "Once I fell into the clutches of a jnani, who made me listen to Vedanta for eleven months. But he couldn't altogether destroy the seed of bhakti in me. No matter where my mind wandered, it would come back to the Divine Mother." Totapuri was astonished when Ramakrishna attained in a single day what it had taken him decades of strenuous practice to achieve. Totapuri asked Ramakrishna to let him go because an orthodox monk of his type, who wanders from place to place, would normally never stay anywhere more than three days; however, he ended up staying at Dakshineshwar for eleven months, for, as Swami Nikhilananda says, "He too had something to learn."

13 | The woman known as the Brahmani (meaning a woman of the brahmin caste), a middle-aged adept of the Tantric and Vaishnava traditions, was Ramakrishna's first teacher. She guided him, over a period of three or four years, through the direct experience that *all* aspects of life are manifestations of the Divine Mother. The Brahmani was the first to proclaim Ramakrishna an avatar, and at her request two prominent scholars were consulted and asked to evaluate the claim based on scriptural principles. (See n. 3, p. 168.) They agreed that Sri Ramakrishna's visions and other spiritual manifestations were signs of holiness, not madness, and proclaimed him an incarnation comparable to Rama, Krishna, Buddha, and Chaitanya. Ramakrishna greeted the pronouncement with childlike indifference, saying, "Well, I am glad to learn that after all it is not a disease."

"God alone dwells inside this body. Such renunciation of 'woman' and 'gold'! Could I have accomplished that myself? I have never enjoyed a woman even in a dream.

"Nangta[12] instructed me in Vedanta. In three days I went into samadhi. At the sight of my samadhi under the madhavi vine, he was quite taken aback and exclaimed, 'Ah! What is this?' Then he came to know who resides in this body. He said to me, 'Please let me go.' At these words of Totapuri I went into an ecstatic mood and said, 'You cannot go till I realize the truth of Vedanta.'

"Day and night I lived with him. We talked only Vedanta. The Brahmani[13] often said to me: 'Don't listen to Vedanta. It will spoil your devotion to God.'

"I said to the Divine Mother: 'Mother, please get me a rich man. If you don't, how shall I be able to protect this body? How shall I be able to keep the sadhus and devotees near me?' That is why Mathur Babu provided for my needs for fourteen years.

(continued on page 185)

14 Gauranga is another name for Chaitanya. See n. 3 on p. 4. According to the Bengali school of Vaishnavism, Krishna once assumed an incarnation in which he and Radha coexisted as one person, in order to enjoy his own charm and sweetness as Radha did. This form is known as Sri Gauranga.

15 The *kuthi* is a bungalow where Rani Rasmani and her family used to stay when they visited Dakshineshwar.

16 *Karma yoga* is the path of action. It may take the form of selfless service of humanity (including social and political work), but the essence of it is working without attachment to the results of one's efforts. One performs actions wholeheartedly, yet without a sense of being the "doer."

17 Guru Nanak (1469–1539) was the founder of Sikhism, which unites Hindu devotion with Islamic Sufism.

"He who dwells in me tells me beforehand what particular class of devotees will come to me. When I have a vision of Gauranga,[14] I know that devotees of Gauranga are coming. When I have a vision of Kali, the Shaktas come.

"At the time of the evening service I used to cry out from the roof of the kuthi,[15] weeping: 'Oh, where are you all? Come to me!' You see, they are all gathering here, one by one.

"I have practiced all kinds of sadhana: jnana yoga, karma yoga,[16] and bhakti yoga. I have even gone through the exercises of hatha yoga to increase longevity. There is another Person dwelling in this body. Otherwise, after attaining samadhi, how could I live with the devotees and enjoy the love of God? Koar Singh used to say to me: 'I have never before seen a person who has returned from the plane of samadhi. You are none other than Nanak.'[17]

"I live in the midst of worldly people; on all sides I see 'woman' and 'gold.' Nevertheless, this is the state of my mind: unceasing samadhi and bhava. That is the reason Pratap said, at the sight of my ecstatic mood: 'Good heavens! It is as if he were possessed by a ghost!'"

Rakhal, M, and the others were speechless as they drank in this account of Sri Ramakrishna's unique experiences.

[400–406]

1 Around mid-1885, Sri Ramakrishna had begun to have symptoms of a sore throat that was later diagnosed as cancer. Despite his worsening condition, he continued to meet with spiritual seekers and his disciples, who, along with his wife, Sarada Devi, cared for him devotedly. He was also examined by several doctors. Dr. Mahendralal Sarkar, a prominent homeopath from Calcutta, was chosen to treat him. Although Dr. Sarkar was a skeptical man of science, he was open-minded and fascinated by the Master, who treated him with affection.

22 □ Mad with Love

The conversation was going on, when Dr. Sarkar came into the room and took a seat. He said to the Master: "I woke up at three this morning, greatly worried that you might catch cold. Oh, I thought many other things about you."

MASTER: "I have been coughing and my throat is sore.[1] In the small hours of the morning my mouth was filled with water. My whole body is aching."

DOCTOR: "Yes, I heard all about it this morning.". . .

Dr. Sarkar inquired if anybody would sing that day.

MASTER (to Narendra): "Why don't you sing a little?"

Narendra sang:

> Mother, make me mad with Thy love.
> What need have I of knowledge or reason?
> Make me drunk with Thy love's wine;
> O Thou who stealest Thy bhaktas' hearts,
> Drown me deep in the sea of Thy love!
> Here in this world, this madhouse of Thine,
> Some laugh, some weep, some dance for joy:
> Jesus, Buddha, Moses, Gauranga,
> All are drunk with the wine of Thy love.
> Mother, when shall I be blessed
> By joining their blissful company?

(continued on page 189)

⊚ Ecstasy—a transcendent condition in which the boundaries of the separate self are dissolved, but without loss of awareness—is a universal human experience found in all cultures. What differs is the religious interpretation that various traditions ascribe to the experience and the methods they use to facilitate it. In the *bhakti* movements of Hinduism, devotional singing (called *kirtan* or *bhajan*) is one of the primary ways of inducing the intoxication of divine love. (For Sri Ramakrishna, of course, there was no need of particular methods to send him into ecstasy—he entered *samadhi* several times a day over many years!)

A strange transformation came over the devotees. They all became mad, as it were, with divine ecstasy. The pundit stood up, forgetting the pride of his scholarship, and cried:

Mother, make me mad with Thy love.
What need have I of knowledge or reason?

Vijay was the first on his feet, carried away by divine intoxication. Then Sri Ramakrishna stood up, forgetting all about his painful and fatal illness. The doctor, who had been sitting in front of him, also stood up. Both patient and physician forgot themselves in the spell created by Narendra's music. The younger Naren and Latu went into deep samadhi. The atmosphere of the room became electric. Everyone felt the presence of God. Dr. Sarkar, eminent scientist that he was, stood breathless, watching this strange scene. He noticed that the devotees who had gone into samadhi were utterly unconscious of the outer world. All were motionless and transfixed. After a while, as they came down a little to the plane of the relative world, some laughed and some wept. An outsider, entering the room, would have thought that a number of drunkards were assembled there.

A little later Sri Ramakrishna resumed his conversation, the devotees taking their seats. It was about eight o'clock in the evening.

MASTER: "You have just noticed the effect of divine ecstasy. What does your 'science' say about that? Do you think it is a mere hoax?"

DOCTOR (to the Master): "I must say that this is all natural, when so many people have experienced it. It cannot be a hoax. (To Narendra) When you sang the lines:

Mother, make me mad with Thy love;
What need have I of knowledge or reason?

I could hardly control myself. I was about to jump to my feet. With great difficulty I suppressed myself. I said to myself, 'No, I must not display my feelings.'"

12 A large elephant entering a small pool with a big splash is likened to the situation of people who cannot contain their spiritual emotions; they make a big outward display of devotional or ecstatic feelings. The implication is that their "receptacle," or capacity for spiritual experience, is very small. By contrast, more spiritually mature people, even if the feelings within them are very intense, will show little or no outer sign of emotion. This is likened to a large elephant plunging into a big lake, barely causing a ripple. Sri Ramakrishna teasingly suggests that behind his worldly, skeptical façade, Dr. Sarkar is actually a person of great spiritual capacity, since he contained his emotions while the others were enraptured.

MASTER *(with a smile, to the doctor)*: "You are unshakable and motionless, like Mount Sumeru. You are a very deep soul. If an elephant enters a small pool, there is a splashing of water on all sides. But this does not happen when it plunges into a big lake; hardly anyone notices it."**2**

DOCTOR: "Nobody can beat you in talk!" *(Laughter.)*

[433–36]

1 The disciples formed various opinions regarding the reason why Sri Ramakrishna should have to suffer pain and illness like an ordinary man. Some felt that since a divine incarnation could not be subject to karma (the consequences of previous actions) of his own, Sri Ramakrishna must have become ill by taking on the karma of those who had surrendered to him. Narendra, however, refused to accept that the Master's illness was a supernatural phenomenon. Instead, he believed that God, in taking form as a human being, had assumed all the frailties of human life in a most natural way.

Swami Nikhilananda writes: "One day the Master was told by a scholar that he could instantly cure himself of his illness by concentrating his mind on his throat. This Sri Ramakrishna refused to do since he could never withdraw his mind from God. But at Naren's repeated request, the Master agreed to speak to the Divine Mother about his illness. A little later he said to the disciple in a sad voice: 'Yes, I told Her that I could not swallow any food on account of the sore in my throat and asked Her to do something about it. But the Mother said, pointing to you all, "Why, are you not eating enough through all these mouths?" I felt so humiliated that I could not utter another word.' Narendra realized how Sri Ramakrishna applied in life the Vedantic idea of the oneness of existence and also came to know that only through such realization could one rise above the pain and suffering of the individual life."

23 □ "What a Vision!"

Sri Ramakrishna sat facing the north in the large room upstairs. It was evening. He was very ill. Narendra and Rakhal were gently massaging his feet. M sat near by. The Master, by a sign, asked him, too, to stroke his feet. M obeyed.

The previous Sunday the devotees had observed Sri Ramakrishna's birthday with worship and prayer. His birthday the year before had been celebrated at Dakshineshwar with great pomp; but this year, on account of his illness,[1] the devotees were very sad and there was no festivity at all.

The Holy Mother busied herself day and night in the Master's service. Among the young disciples, Narendra, Rakhal, Niranjan, Sarat, Sashi, Baburam, Jogin, Latu, and Kali had been staying with him at the garden house. The older devotees visited him daily, and some of them occasionally spent the night there.

That day Sri Ramakrishna was feeling very ill. At midnight the moon was flooding the garden with light, but it could wake no response in the devotees' hearts. They were drowned in a sea of grief. They felt that they were living in a beautiful city besieged by a hostile army. Perfect silence reigned everywhere. Nature was still, except for the gentle rustling of the leaves at the touch of the south wind. Sri Ramakrishna lay awake. One or two devotees sat near him in silence. At times he seemed to doze.

M was seated by his side. Sri Ramakrishna asked him, by a sign, to come nearer. The sight of his suffering was unbearable. In a very soft voice and with great difficulty he said to M:

⌨ "The body has, indeed, only a momentary existence. God alone is real. Now the body exists, and now it does not. Years ago, when I had been suffering terribly from indigestion, Hriday said to me, 'Do ask the Mother to cure you.' I felt ashamed to speak to Her about my illness. I said to Her: 'Mother, I saw a skeleton in the Asiatic Society Museum. It was pieced together with wires into a human form. O Mother, please keep my body together a little, like that, so that I may sing Thy name and glories.'"

—Sri Ramakrishna *[294]*

"I have borne so much suffering for fear of making you all weep. But if you all say: 'Oh, there is so much suffering! Let the body go,' then I can give up the body."

These words pierced the devotees' hearts. And he who was their father, mother, and protector had uttered these words. What could they say? All sat in silence. Some thought, "Is this another crucifixion—the sacrifice of the body for the sake of the devotees?"

It was the dead of night. Sri Ramakrishna's illness was taking a turn for the worse. The devotees wondered what was to be done. One of them left for Calcutta. That very night Girish came to the garden house with two physicians, Upendra and Navagopal.

The devotees sat near the Master. He felt a little better and said to them: "The illness is of the body. That is as it should be; I see that the body is made of the five elements."

Turning to Girish, he said: "I am seeing many forms of God. Among them I find this one also [meaning his own form]."...

MASTER (to the devotees): "Do you know what I see right now? I see that it is God Himself who has become all this. It seems to me that men and other living beings are made of leather and that it is God Himself who, dwelling inside these leather cases, moves the hands, the feet, the heads. I had a similar vision once before, when I saw houses, gardens, roads, men, cattle—all made of one substance; it was as if they were all made of wax.

"I see that it is God Himself who has become the block, the executioner, and the victim for the sacrifice."

As he described this staggering experience, in which he realized in full the identity of all within the One Being, he was overwhelmed with emotion and exclaimed, "Ah! What a vision!"

Immediately Sri Ramakrishna went into samadhi. He completely forgot his body and the outer world. The devotees were bewildered. Not knowing what to do, they sat still.

"God becomes man, an Avatar, and comes to earth with His devotees. . . . A band of God's troubadours suddenly appears, dances and sings, and departs in the same sudden manner. They come and they return, but none recognizes them."

—Sri Ramakrishna *[479]*

Presently the Master regained partial consciousness of the world and said: "Now I have no pain at all. I am my old self again."

The devotees were amazed to watch this state of the Master, beyond pleasure and pain, weal and woe. . . .

Sri Ramakrishna looked at the devotees, and his love for them welled up in a thousand streams.

[475–77]

Sri Ramakrishna passed away five months later, on Sunday, August 15, 1886.

Notes ☐

Where applicable, citations are keyed to annotation numbers. To find complete facts of publication for citations given in short form, see "Suggested Readings."

Epigraph

"Wherever you are . . . ": Linda Hess and Shukdev Singh, trans. *A Touch of Grace: Songs of Kabir* (Boston: Shambhala Publications, 1994), 21.

Introduction

"In the first place, the sun requires. . . ": Vivekananda, *Living at the Source: Yoga Teachings of Vivekananda,* edited by Ann Myren and DorothyMadison (Boston: Shambhala Publications, 1993), 35.

1. He Was Talking of God

13. "Not in the usual way . . . ": Isherwood, 123.

2. Keep Holy Company

1. "His shorthand . . . ": Hixon, xiii. "Man and gold," *The Gospel of Sri Ramakrishna,* abridged ed., 128n.

3. God Is in the Tiger

5. Vivekananda, *The Yogas and Other Works,* rev. ed. (New York: Ramakrishna-Vivekananda Center, 1953), 636–37.

4. Knowledge of Brahman

6. The definition of *ananda* is from Georg Feuerstein, *The Shambhala Encyclopedia of Yoga* (Boston: Shambhala Publications, 1997), 246.

7. *The Gospel of Sri Ramakrishna,* unabridged ed., 196.

10. Ibid., 416n.
14. Hixon, 179.

5. Worldly Duties

"Japa means silently...": *The Gospel of Sri Ramakrishna,* unabridged ed., 878–79.
  7. Hixon, 278. Vivekananda, "Raja-Yoga," in *The Yogas and Other Works,* rev. ed. (New York: Ramakrishna-Vivekananda Center, 1953), 220–21.

6. A Feast of Joy

  3. *The Gospel of Sri Ramakrishna,* unabridged ed., 134.

7. "Where Is My Krishna?"

  5. *The Gospel of Sri Ramakrishna,* unabridged ed., 658.

8. Play of the Divine Mother

  6. *The Gospel of Sri Ramakrishna,* unabridged ed., 225.
  8. Ibid., 196.
 11. Vivekananda, *The Yogas and Other Works,* rev. ed. (New York: Ramakrishna-Vivekananda Center, 1953), 761.
 15. Vivekananda, *Living at the Source: Yoga Teachings of Vivekananda,* edited by Ann Myren and Dorothy Madison (Boston: Shambhala Publications, 1993), 87–88.

9. Dive Deep

 10. Shankaracharya, *Crest-Jewel of Discrimination (Viveka-chudamani),* translated by Swami Prabhavananda and Christopher Isherwood (Hollywood: Vedanta Press, 1947), 33.
"The spinal column is said. . . ": Isherwood, 64.

10. The Spirit of Renunciation

"Worldly people will never listen. . . ": *The Gospel of Sri Ramakrishna,* unabridged ed., 146.

11. "I Am the Servant of God"

  6. *The Gospel of Sri Ramakrishna,* unabridged ed., 155.
  8. Swami Nikhilananda in *The Gospel of Sri Ramakrishna,* abridged ed., 38–39.

12. Realizing God

"It has been recognized. . . ": Vivekananda, *Living at the Source: Yoga Teachings of Vivekananda,* edited by Ann Myren and Dorothy Madison (Boston: Shambhala Publications, 1993), 40–41.

15. What Is the Way?

"Through unselfish action. . . ": *The Gospel of Sri Ramakrishna,* unabridged ed., 895.

16. Reading, Hearing, and Seeing

4. *The Gospel of Sri Ramakrishna,* unabridged ed., 1036.
5. "Mansion of mirth": *The Gospel of Sri Ramakrishna,* unabridged ed., 139.
6. *The Gospel of Sri Ramakrishna,* unabridged ed., 139.

17. Desire

1. Vivekananda, "Jnana-Yoga," in *The Yogas and Other Works,* rev. ed. (New York: Ramakrishna-Vivekananda Center, 1953), 322.
2. *The Gospel of Sri Ramakrishna,* abridged ed., 506.

18. Practicing the Disciplines

2. Translation of *tantra* as "continuum": Georg Feuerstein, *Tantra: The Path of Ecstasy* (Boston: Shambhala Publications, 1998), 2; Isherwood, 101, 102.

20. To Receive God's Grace

3. *The Gospel of Sri Ramakrishna,* unabridged ed., 19–20.
"Sri Ramakrishna said. . . ": Vivekananda, *The Yogas and Other Works,* rev. ed. (New York: Ramakrishna-Vivekananda Center, 1953), 516.

21. Something Special

11. *The Gospel of Sri Ramakrishna,* unabridged ed., 779.
12. "Once I fell into the clutches. . . ": ibid., 19. "He too had something to learn": ibid., 29.

23. "What a Vision!"

1. Swami Nikhilananda, in Vivekananda, *The Yogas and Other Works,* rev. ed. (New York: Ramakrishna-Vivekananda Center, 1953), 32.

Suggested Readings

Advaita Ashrama staff. *The Life of Sri Ramakrishna* (1929). Mayavati and Calcutta: Advaita Ashrama, 1994. A comprehensive account of the Master's life and message.

Gambhirananda, Swami, comp. and ed. *The Apostles of Ramakrishna* (1966). Calcutta: Advaita Ashrama, 1995. A collection of biographies on the monastic disciples of Sri Ramakrishna.

Hixon, Lex. *Great Swan: Meetings with Ramakrishna.* Boston: Shambhala Publications, 1992. Reprint: Larson Publications, 1997. This freely rendered version based on the Nikhilananda translation is beautifully written and incorporates helpful interpretations as well as material derived from the biography of Ramakrishna's wife, Sarada Devi.

Isherwood, Christopher. *Ramakrishna and His Disciples.* Hollywood: Vedanta Press, 1965. This engaging biography, by the famous British writer who was a disciple of Swami Prabhavananda of the Ramakrishna Order, is an excellent introduction.

Majumdar, Sachindra Kumar, trans. *Conversations with Sri Ramakrishna.* Greenville, N.Y.: Sarada Ramakrishna Vivekananda Association of America, 2000. CD-ROM of an alternative translation of *Sri Sri Ramakrishna Kathamrita.* Although the language is not as polished as Swami Nikhilananda's, the nonchronological organization reflects M's original five volumes.

Nikhilananda, Swami. *Holy Mother: Being the Life of Sri Sarada Devi, Wife of Sri Ramakrishna and Helpmate in His Mission.* New York: Ramakrishna-Vivekananda Center, 1962. Recommended as an introductory biography.

———, trans. *The Gospel of Sri Ramakrishna.* New York: Ramakrishna-Vivekananda Center, 1942. The original, unabridged translation.

———, trans. and ed. *The Gospel of Sri Ramakrishna.* Abridged ed. New York: Ramakrishna-Vivekananda Center, 1958. Swami Nikhilananda edited this version of the *Gospel,* which is not only shorter but also easier to read because it has fewer foreign terms and references to Indian customs and culture that are unfamiliar to most Westerners.

Rolland, Romain. *The Life of Sri Ramakrishna* (1924). Mayavati and Calcutta: Advaita Ashrama, 1995. A biography and interpretation by a well-known French literary figure.

Saradananda, Swami. *Sri Ramakrishna: The Great Master.* Translated by Swami Jagadananda. 2 vols. Hollywood: Vedanta Press, 1998. The most comprehensive biography available, written by one of his foremost disciples.

Schiffman, Richard. *Sri Ramakrishna: A Prophet of the New Age.* New York: Paragon House, 1989. This biography by a commentator for National Public Radio emphasizes the practical applications of the Master's teachings.

List of Special Terms ☐

Below are brief definitions or translations of selected foreign terms and names. Following proper nouns (names of historical persons, deities, sects, and titles of scriptures), a brief description is given in parentheses. Entries are indexed by page number, directing you to the full definition or reference of major terms in the book.

adharma, unrighteousness, 82
Advaita (Vedanta philosophy of non-dualism), 30, 36
ahamkara, I-consciousness, 60
ajna, "third-eye" chakra, 174
akasha, ether, 174
anahata, heart chakra, 174
ananda, bliss, 34
Atman, Self, 72
avatar, divine incarnation, xix
avidya, ignorance, 30
Baburam (disciple of Ramakrishna), 62
Balaram (devotee of Ramakrishna), 162
Bhagavad Gita (scripture), 44
Bhagavan, Lord, 72
Bhagavata Purana (scripture), 4
bhakta, devotee, 36, 74
bhakti, devotion, 50
bhakti yoga, path of love, 38
bhava, devotional attitude, 8, 118
bhava-mukha, threshold between absolute and relative consciousness, 150
Bhavanath (devotee of Ramakrishna), 62
Bhavatarini (name for Kali), 6

Brahma (creator deity), 50
brahmachari/brahmacharin, celibate student, 22, 50
Brahman, the Absolute, 30
Brahmananda (swami), 62
Brahmani (guru of Ramakrishna), 182
Brahmo Samaj (Hindu reform movement), 18
buddhi, intellect, 60, 132
Chaitanya (avatar of Radha-Krishna), 4
chakra, energy center, 174
chitta, "mind-stuff," 132
dharma, truth, duty, 82, 200
Durga (goddess), 62
Gangamayi (saint), 8
Gauranga (name for Chaitanya), 184
Gauri (pundit), 168
Girish (devotee of Ramakrishna), 162
gunas, qualities, 42
guru, teacher, 140
Hanuman (monkey god), 44
Hari (epithet for Vishnu), 4
Hazra (devotee of Ramakrishna), 168
Holy Mother (name for Sarada Devi), 56
Hriday (nephew), 66

japa, repetition, 52
jivanmukta, one liberated while in the
    body, 110
jivatman, embodied soul, 74
jnana, wisdom, 40
jnana yoga, path of knowledge, 40
jnani, "knower," 40
Kabir (poet-saint), 96
Kali (the Divine Mother), xviii
Kali Yuga, dark age, 38
kamini-kanchan, "woman and gold,"
    12
karma yoga, path of action, 184
Keshab (Brahmo Samaj leader), 18
Krishna (avatar), 4
kundalini, "serpent power," 174
Lakshmi (goddess), 166
lila, divine play, 150
madhura bhava, sweet mood, 118
Mahamaya, great illusion, 54, 138
mahasiddhis, occult powers, 164
mahatma, great soul, 26
manas, mind, 60
manipura, navel chakra, 174
mantra, sacred word or syllable, 22
Mathur (temple manager), 54
maya, principle of illusion, 54, 58, 138
muladhara, base-of-spine chakra, 174
Nanak (founder of Sikhism), 184
Nangta (guru of Ramakrishna), 182
Narada (sage), 26
Narayana (epithet for Vishnu), 166
Narendranath/Narendra/Naren
    (disciple of Ramakrishna), 18, 102,
    180
neti, neti, "not this, not this," 40
Nikhilananda (swami), xv
Nirguna Brahman, God without quali-
    ties, 40
Om, a mantra, 4
paramahamsa, "great swan," 2
Paramatman, Supreme Soul, 74
Prakriti, Nature, 60

prana, vital energy, 174
prema, ecstatic love, 131
Premananda (swami), 62
puja, worship, 50
Puranas (scriptures), 156
Purusha, Self, 60
Radha (Krishna's beloved), 58
Radha-Krishna (lover and Beloved in
    one), 6, 184
rajas, activity, 42, 154
Rakhal (disciple of Ramakrishna), 62
Rama (avatar), 4
Rani Rasmani (temple patron), 6
rishi, seer, 36
sadhana, spiritual practice, 156
sadhu, monk, 6
Saguna Brahman, God with qualities,
    40
sahasrara, crown chakra, 174
samadhi, absorption, 34
Samkhya (a Hindu philosophy), 60
sandhya, worship, 4
sannyasin, renouncer, 6, 158
Sarada Devi (wife of Ramakrishna), 56
Sarkar (Ramakrishna's doctor), 186
Satchidananda, Existence-Knowledge-
    Bliss, 34
sattva, tranquillity, 42
Shaiva (devotee of Shiva), 6
Shakta (devotee of the Goddess), 6
Shakti (goddess; feminine principle), 58
Shankaracharya (founder of Advaita
    Vedanta), 36
Shashadhar, Pundit (devotee of
    Ramakrishna), 146
Shiva (destroyer deity; god of
    renunciation), 6
Shivanath (Brahmo Samaj leader), 54
So'Ham, a mantra, 48
sushumna, a subtle energy channel,
    174
svadhisthana, sexual organs chakra,
    174

tamas, inertia, 42

Tantra (scripture or teaching of
   Tantrism), 156

Totapuri (guru of Ramakrishna), 182

Upanishads (scriptures), 140

Vaishnava/Vaishnavism (sect of
   devotees of Vishnu), 50

Vedanta (a philosophy based on the
   Upanishads), 140

Vedantin, follower of Vedanta, 32

Vedas (scriptures), 32, 36

vichara, inquiry, 132

vidya, knowledge, 30

Vijay (Brahmo Samaj leader), 70

vijnana, understanding, 40

vijnani, "understander," 40

Vishnu (preserver deity), 6

visuddha, throat chakra, 174

Vivekananda (disciple of
   Ramakrishna). *See* Narendranath

Yoga (a system of spiritual disciplines;
   a Hindu philosophy), 48

yogi, a practitioner of yoga, 48

About SKYLIGHT PATHS Publishing

SkyLight Paths Publishing is creating a place where people of different spiritual traditions come together for challenge and inspiration, a place where we can help each other understand the mystery that lies at the heart of our existence.

Through spirituality, our religious beliefs are increasingly becoming a part of our lives—rather than *apart* from our lives. While many of us may be more interested than ever in spiritual growth, we may be less firmly planted in traditional religion. Yet, we do want to deepen our relationship to the sacred, to learn from our own as well as from other faith traditions, and to practice in new ways.

SkyLight Paths sees both believers and seekers as a community that increasingly transcends traditional boundaries of religion and denomination—people wanting to learn from each other, *walking together, finding the way.*

We at SkyLight Paths take great care to produce beautiful books that present meaningful spiritual content in a form that reflects the art of making high quality books. Therefore, we want to acknowledge those who contributed to the production of this book.

PRODUCTION
Tim Holtz, Martha McKinney & Bridgett Taylor

EDITORIAL
Amanda Dupuis, Polly Short Mahoney,
Lauren Seidman & Emily Wichland

COVER DESIGN
Walter C. Bumford III, Stockton, Massachusetts

TEXT DESIGN
Chelsea Cloeter, Tucson, Arizona

PRINTING & BINDING
Versa Press, East Peoria, Illinois

Other Interesting Books—Spirituality

Lighting the Lamp of Wisdom: *A Week Inside an Ashram*
by *John Ittner*

This insider's guide to Hindu spiritual life takes you into a typical week of retreat inside an ashram to demystify the ashram experience and show you what to expect from your own visit. Includes a discussion of worship services, meditation and yoga classes, chanting and music, work practice, and more.
6 x 9, 224 pp, b/w photographs, Quality PB Original, ISBN 1-893361-52-7 **$15.95**;
HC, ISBN 1-893361-37-3 **$24.95**

Waking Up: *A Week Inside a Zen Monastery*
by *Jack Maguire*; Foreword by *John Daido Loori, Roshi*

An essential guide to what it's like to spend a week inside a Zen Buddhist monastery.
6 x 9, 224 pp, b/w photographs, HC, ISBN 1-893361-13-6 **$21.95**

  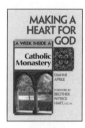 

Making a Heart for God: *A Week Inside a Catholic Monastery*
by *Dianne Aprile*; Foreword by *Brother Patrick Hart*, OCSO

This essential guide to experiencing life in a Catholic monastery takes us to the Abbey of Gethsemani—the Trappist monastery in Kentucky that was home to author Thomas Merton—to explore the details. "More balanced and informative than the popular *The Cloister Walk* by Kathleen Norris." —*Choice: Current Reviews for Academic Libraries*
6 x 9, 224 pp, b/w photographs, Quality PB, ISBN 1-893361-49-7 **$16.95**;
HC, ISBN 1-893361-14-4 **$21.95**

Come and Sit: *A Week Inside Meditation Centers*
by *Marcia Z. Nelson*; Foreword by *Wayne Teasdale*

The insider's guide to meditation in a variety of different spiritual traditions. Traveling through Buddhist, Hindu, Christian, Jewish, and Sufi traditions, this essential guide takes the reader to different meditation centers to meet the teachers and students and learn about the practices, demystifying the meditation experience for people of all levels.
6 x 9, 224 pp, b/w photographs, Quality PB Original, ISBN 1-893361-35-7 **$16.95**

Or phone, fax, mail or e-mail to: SKYLIGHT PATHS Publishing
Sunset Farm Offices, Route 4 • P.O. Box 237 • Woodstock, Vermont 05091
Tel: (802) 457-4000   Fax: (802) 457-4004   www.skylightpaths.com
Credit card orders: (800) 962-4544 (9AM–5PM ET Monday–Friday)
Generous discounts on quantity orders. SATISFACTION GUARANTEED. Prices subject to change.

SkyLight Illuminations Series
Andrew Harvey, series editor

Offers today's spiritual seeker an enjoyable entry into the great classic texts of the world's spiritual traditions. Each classic is presented in an accessible translation, with facing pages of guided commentary from experts, giving you the keys you need to understand the history, context, and meaning of the text. This series enables readers of all backgrounds to experience and understand classic spiritual texts directly, and to make them a part of their lives.

The Way of a Pilgrim: *Annotated & Explained*
Translation and annotation by *Gleb Pokrovsky*;
Foreword by *Andrew Harvey*, SkyLight Illuminations series editor

The classic of Russian spirituality—now with facing-page commentary that illuminates and explains the text for you.

This delightful account is the story of one man who sets out to learn the prayer of the heart—also known as the "Jesus prayer"—and how the practice transforms his existence. This SkyLight Illuminations edition guides you through an abridged version of the text with facing-page annotations explaining the names, terms and references.
5½ x 8½, 160 pp, Quality PB, ISBN 1-893361-31-4 **$14.95**

Bhagavad Gita: *Annotated & Explained*
Translation by *Shri Purohit Swami*; Annotation by *Kendra Crossen Burroughs*;
Foreword by *Andrew Harvey*, SkyLight Illuminations series editor

"The very best Gita for first-time readers." —Ken Wilber

Millions of people turn daily to India's most beloved holy book, whose universal appeal has made it popular with non-Hindus and Hindus alike. This SkyLight Illuminations edition of the Gita introduces readers to the characters; explains references and philosophical terms; shares the interpretations of famous spiritual leaders and scholars; and more.
5½ x 8½, 192 pp, Quality PB, ISBN 1-893361-28-4 **$15.95**

SkyLight Illuminations Series
Andrew Harvey, series editor

Zohar: *Annotated & Explained*
Translation and annotation by *Daniel C. Matt*

The cornerstone text of Kabbalah, now with facing-page commentary that illuminates and explains the text for you.

The best-selling author of *The Essential Kabbalah* brings together in one place that most important teachings of the *Zohar,* the canonical text of the Jewish mystical tradition. Guides readers step by step through the midrash, mystical fantasy and Hebrew scripture that make up the *Zohar,* explaining the inner meanings in facing-page commentary. Ideal for readers without any prior knowledge of Jewish mysticism.

5½ x 8½, 176 pp, Quality PB Original, ISBN 1-893361-51-9 **$15.95**

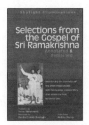

Selections from the Gospel of Sri Ramakrishna: *Annotated & Explained*
Translated by *Swami Nikhilananda*; Annotations by *Kendra Crossen Burroughs*

The words of India's greatest example of God-consciousness and mystical ecstasy in recent history—now with facing-page commentary that illuminates and explains the text for you.

Introduces the fascinating world of the Indian mystic and the universal appeal of his message that has inspired millions of devotees for more than a century. Selections from the original text—originally recorded in Bengali by M, a disciple of the Master—and insightful yet unobtrusive commentary highlight the most important and inspirational teachings. Ideal for readers without any prior knowledge of Hinduism.

5½ x 8½, 240 pp, b/w photographs, Quality PB Original, ISBN 1-893361-46-2 **$16.95**

Dhammapada: *Annotated & Explained*
Translation by *Max Müller*; Annotation by *Jack Maguire*;
Foreword by *Andrew Harvey*, SkyLight Illuminations series editor

The classic of Buddhist spiritual practice—now with facing-page commentary that illuminates and explains the text for you.

The Dhammapada—words spoken by the Buddha himself over 2,500 years ago—is notoriously difficult to understand for the first-time reader. Now you can experience the Dhammapada with understanding even if you have no previous knowledge of Buddhism. Enlightening facing-page commentary explains all the names, terms and references, giving you deeper insight into the text. An excellent introduction to Buddhist life and practice.

5½ x 8½, 160 pp, Quality PB, ISBN 1-893361-42-X **$14.95**

Spirituality

Inspired Lives: *Exploring the Role of Faith and Spirituality in the Lives of Extraordinary People*

by *Joanna Laufer* and *Kenneth S. Lewis*

Contributors include *Ang Lee, Wynton Marsalis, Kathleen Norris,* and many more

How faith transforms the lives and work of the creative and innovative people in our world.

In this moving book, soul-searching conversations unearth the importance of spirituality and personal faith for more than forty artists and innovators who have made a real difference in our world through their work. 6 x 9, 256 pp, Quality PB, ISBN 1-893361-33-0 **$16.95**

Women Pray
Voices through the Ages, from Many Faiths, Cultures, and Traditions

Edited and with introductions by *Monica Furlong*

Many ways—new and old—to communicate with the Divine.

This beautiful gift book celebrates the rich variety of ways women around the world have called out to the Divine—with words of joy, praise, gratitude, wonder, petition, longing, and even anger—from the ancient world up to our own time. Prayers from women of nearly every religious or spiritual background give us an eloquent expression of what it means to communicate with God. 5 x 7¼, 256 pp, Deluxe HC with ribbon marker, ISBN 1-893361-25-X **$19.95**

 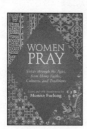  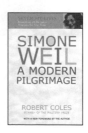

Zen Effects: *The Life of Alan Watts*

by *Monica Furlong*

The first and only full-length biography of one of the most charismatic spiritual leaders of the twentieth century—now back in print!

Through his widely popular books and lectures, Alan Watts (1915–1973) did more to introduce Eastern philosophy and religion to Western minds than any figure before or since. Here is the only biography of this charismatic figure, who served as Zen teacher, Anglican priest, lecturer, academic, entertainer, a leader of the San Francisco renaissance, and author of more than 30 books, including *The Way of Zen, Psychotherapy East and West* and *The Spirit of Zen.* 6 x 9, 264 pp, Quality PB, ISBN 1-893361-32-2 **$16.95**

Simone Weil: *A Modern Pilgrimage*

by *Robert Coles*

The extraordinary life of the spiritual philosopher who's been called both saint and madwoman.

The French writer and philosopher Simone Weil (1906–1943) devoted her life to a search for God—while avoiding membership in organized religion. Robert Coles' intriguing study of Weil details her short, eventful life, and is an insightful portrait of the beloved and controversial thinker whose life and writings influenced many (from T. S. Eliot to Adrienne Rich to Albert Camus), and continue to inspire seekers everywhere. 6 x 9, 208 pp, Quality PB, ISBN 1-893361-34-9 **$16.95**

Spirituality

Three Gates to Meditation Practice
A Personal Journey into Sufism, Buddhism, and Judaism
by *David A. Cooper*

Shows us how practicing within more than one spiritual tradition can lead us to our true home.

Here are over fifteen years from the journey of "post-denominational rabbi" David A. Cooper, author of *God Is a Verb*, and his wife, Shoshana—years in which the Coopers explored a rich variety of practices, from chanting Sufi *dhikr* to Buddhist Vipassanā meditation, to the study of kabbalah and esoteric Judaism. Their experience demonstrates that the spiritual path is really completely within our reach, whoever we are, whatever we do—as long as we are willing to practice it. 5½ x 8½, 240 pp, Quality PB, ISBN 1-893361-22-5 **$16.95**

Praying with Our Hands: *Twenty-One Practices of Embodied Prayer from the World's Spiritual Traditions*
by *Jon M. Sweeney;* Photographs by *Jennifer J. Wilson;*
Foreword by *Mother Tessa Bielecki*; Afterword by *Taitetsu Unno, Ph.D.*

A spiritual guidebook for bringing prayer into our bodies.

This inspiring book of reflections and accompanying photographs shows us twenty-one simple ways of using our hands to speak to God, to enrich our devotion and ritual. All express the various approaches of the world's religious traditions to bringing the body into worship. Spiritual traditions represented include Anglican, Sufi, Zen, Roman Catholic, Yoga, Shaker, Hindu, Jewish, Pentecostal, Eastern Orthodox, and many others.
8 x 8, 96 pp, 22 duotone photographs, Quality PB Original, ISBN 1-893361-16-0 **$16.95**

   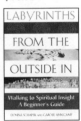

The Sacred Art of Listening
Forty Reflections for Cultivating a Spiritual Practice
by *Kay Lindahl*; Illustrations by *Amy Schnapper*

More than ever before, we need to embrace the skills and practice of listening. You will learn to: Speak clearly from your heart • Communicate with courage and compassion • Heighten your awareness for deep listening • Enhance your ability to listen to people with different belief systems. 8 x 8, 160 pp, Illus., Quality PB Original, ISBN 1-893361-44-6 **$16.95**

Labyrinths from the Outside In
Walking to Spiritual Insight—a Beginner's Guide
by *Donna Schaper* and *Carole Ann Camp*

The user-friendly, interfaith guide to making and using labyrinths— for meditation, prayer, and celebration.

Labyrinth walking is a spiritual exercise *anyone* can do. This accessible guide unlocks the mysteries of the labyrinth for all of us, providing ideas for using the labyrinth walk for prayer, meditation, and celebrations to mark the most important moments in life. Includes instructions for making a labyrinth of your own and finding one in your area.
6 x 9, 208 pp, b/w illus. and photographs, Quality PB Original, ISBN 1-893361-18-7 **$16.95**

Other Interesting Books—Spirituality

God Within: *Our Spiritual Future—As Told by Today's New Adults*
Edited by *Jon M. Sweeney* and *the Editors at SkyLight Paths*

Our faith, in our words.

The future of spirituality in America lies in the vision of the women and men who are the children of the "baby boomer" generation—born into the post-New-Age world of the 1970s and 1980s. This book gives voice to their spiritual energy, and allows readers of all ages to share in their passionate quests for faith and belief. This thought-provoking collection of writings, poetry, and art showcases the voices that are defining the future of religion, faith, and belief as we know it. 6 x 9, 176 pp, Quality PB Original, ISBN 1-893361-15-2 **$14.95**

Releasing the Creative Spirit: *Unleash the Creativity in Your Life*
by *Dan Wakefield*

From the author of *How Do We Know When It's God?*— a practical guide to accessing creative power in every area of your life.

Explodes the myths associated with the creative process and shows how everyone can uncover and develop their natural ability to create. Drawing on religion, psychology, and the arts, Dan Wakefield teaches us that the key to creation of any kind is clarity—of body, mind, and spirit—and he provides practical exercises that each of us can do to access that centered quality that allows creativity to shine. 7 x 10, 256 pp, Quality PB, ISBN 1-893361-36-5 **$16.95**

  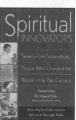

Spiritual Innovators: *Seventy-Five Extraordinary People Who Changed the World in the Past Century*
Edited by *Ira Rifkin and the Editors at SkyLight Paths*; Foreword by *Dr. Robert Coles*

Black Elk, H. H. the Dalai Lama, Mary Baker Eddy, Abraham Joshua Heschel, Krishnamurti, C. S. Lewis, Thomas Merton, Elijah Muhammad, Aimee Semple McPherson, Martin Luther King, Jr., and many more.

Profiles of the most important spiritual leaders of the past one hundred years. An invaluable reference of twentieth-century religion and an inspiring resource for spiritual challenge today. Authoritative list of seventy-five includes mystics and martyrs, intellectuals and charismatics from the East and West. For each, includes a brief biography, inspiring quotes and resources for more in-depth study.
6 x 9, 304 pp, b/w photographs, Quality PB Original, ISBN 1-893361-50-0 **$16.95**;
HC, ISBN 1-893361-43-8 **$24.95**
